About the Author

Lily Trezevant was born in Kent, and after a solid education at the local grammar school, went on to qualify as a science teacher. Now based in Sussex, she has two grownup children, a tortoise and a puppy.

Dedication

For Grace, Sarah and Chris: the silver linings in my clouds.

Lily Trezevant

TREADING WATER

AUSTIN MACAULEY
PUBLISHERS LTD.

A CIP catalogue record for this title is available from the British Library.

ISBN 978 1 78455 762 1 (Paperback)
ISBN 978 1 78455 764 5 (Hardback)

www.austinmacauley.com

First Published (2015)
Austin Macauley Publishers Ltd.
25 Canada Square
Canary Wharf
London
E14 5LB

Printed and bound in Great Britain

Chapter One

Maria had thought that Daniel's funeral would be the worst day of her life so far, but it wasn't: that had already happened.

Functioning on autopilot, she got through the sadness and was so proud of the strength showed by Francesca and Thomas as they gave special tributes to their brother in the packed crematorium. Unlike the funerals of elderly relatives, she really shouldn't have been surprised at the number of young people who had come to say goodbye to Daniel: friends from primary and secondary school; university; his football and cricket clubs. So many vibrant and beautiful young adults ready to reach out into the world.

Surely, the deepest parental sorrow is to have learned your child was dying and you were not there to hold and comfort them. To tell them that you love them and always will: that they are not to be afraid for everyone who loves them is close by.

As his motorbike spun out of control, Daniel was left unconscious and alone, bleeding from severe injuries and found too late for any hope of saving his life.

The unthinkable had happened; Maria's child had predeceased her. Why couldn't she have been there with him? She brought him into this world and should have been allowed to be there as left it. The rage and anger surfaced as the numbness of grief left her. Why did this have to happen to her beautiful boy?

This despairing sense of loss would always be with Maria. Time would not heal her pain only shroud it in a dark cloak of sadness; she would think of Daniel everyday but somehow had to keep her head above water. She had her love for

Francesca and Thomas to sustain her and would get through the days ahead.

There was also Dominic, her wonderful son-in-law who had supported all them in the weeks after Daniel's death. He really had been tower of strength and she was so glad he was part of their family. His understanding of her protectiveness of both Francesca and Thomas was obvious and he was now part of the infrastructure holding them all together. When families close ranks to protect their own, it really is the safest place on earth.

*

It was now nearly five years since Daniel's death; Maria knew what she should do.

An action that didn't need a tortuous sequence of thought to have arrived at: she must put the house on the market; move away and begin again.

Although she had so many happy, long-established memories of days in the family home, the place where she had lived for over 30 years and brought up three her children, traumatic events of recent years had completely drained her; removing vital energy to think positively and remain stable. She knew that to preserve the best of days she needed to stop the good memories being overwhelmed by the bad. To package them up, tie them together with a beautiful silk bow and put them in a safe place.

Reflecting on the calmness and peace she had found at the beach house the previous summer, maybe she should move to the coast? No, she needed to be near Francesca, Thomas and her elderly parents; also her dear friends who had supported her throughout the ordeals of life, as she had them. Maria knew that she didn't have the monopoly on trauma and grief – at times, all families are touched by something which tests them to the limits. Expect the unexpected and hope to survive.

The internet made research easy and knowing the she wanted the minimum effort and upkeep of new build, several options popped up on the screen in her chosen location.

One day in late September when the early morning mists highlighted the amazing intricacies of perfect spiders' webs on the hedges, Maria drove about fifteen miles due east to a new housing development being built in a village called Colthurst Green.

First impressions were encouraging, although it was still very much a building site with phase two of a three phase development only just having been started. The smaller houses which would suit her best were proving the most popular according to the sales girl, so an offer had to be made quickly. A solicitor was instructed and the process of relocation began.

Maria had underestimated the energy needed to deconstruct the family home which had seemed to osmotically absorb so much stuff over the years; accumulated treasures which deserved a thorough last look before consigning to the charity shop or bags for the dump.

Francesca and Thomas had helped her with Daniel's room about six months after his death. It had to be done: her precious child was never coming home and a gradual acceptance of this desolate fact was part of the healing process.

She had placed his sports trophies and medals in a special box, along with some school reports, various things he had made in craft lessons and favourite childhood toys. Now she made up memory boxes with things that had belonged to Francesca and Thomas, including cute cards they had made her, assorted 'artwork' and letters to Father Christmas. Her grandchildren would have fun looking at mummy and daddy's treasures in time.

The mechanics of ruthless decluttering had gone smoothly and the day before her move the house was no longer recognisable as home. Having sold the three piece suite, which was too big to fit in her new house, Maria sat on a deckchair in the living room, knowing that she was doing exactly the right thing at exactly the right time and it's not often that can be said.

The huge pantechnicon was really much too large for transporting her furniture and belongings. The three young removal men seemed happy that this looked to be one of their smaller jobs and they might have an early end to their day for once. Their joshing about and easy banter reminded Maria of the way Daniel, Thomas and Dominic used to enjoy each other's company at the regular Sunday evening meals in the family home. She missed those times.

Chapter Two

Pushing the keys through the letter box after a final goodbye to every room, Maria realised that until the keys of her new home were in her hand, she was technically homeless. The drive to Colthurst Green was full of hope for her future – literally closing one door to open another.

Early May was a good time to be starting over; longer days and warmer weather encouraged forward thinking.

Once the removal lads had finished unloading, with a generous tip in their hands – they really had been so lovely to her, appreciating the constant flow of refreshments during the day – Maria watched them manoeuvre the huge van down the narrow estate road and shutting her shiny, new front door, she immediately felt she was home.

The best thing about the dramatic downsizing was that there were relatively few boxes to unpack. She would take one room at a time (there were only five rooms, six if you counted the downstairs loo) and over the next couple of days, Maria thought the bulk of the work would be done.

With no broadband or television network connected yet, it was a cocoon-like world that she found herself in and it really was quite refreshing not to feel beholden to these commodities. A bit like stepping back into a time before such technology was invented and her days had an altogether more relaxed feel about them.

*

Maria had never had a garden that was completely of her own to do with exactly as she wished. After buying their first house together in the early 1980s, her first husband had staked his claim on the garden and had done a very good job of turning a plot of mud, rubble and assorted lumps of building materials into a lovely green space for Francesca, Thomas and Daniel to play in as they grew up. However, Maria soon realised that if she showed any interest in gardening at that stage, it would swiftly have been added to her list of 'things to do' and she was already at full stretch bringing up three children under seven, running the home and training a puppy.

But that was then and this is now, and she was genuinely excited about planning and designing her own garden of tranquility. Brimming with ideas, she enlisted the guidance of a local garden designer to bring her vision to life.

Firstly, no grass: she definitely didn't want to be dragging lawn mowers around in her dotage. Planting must include acers, blossom trees and bamboo for a Japanese vibe. The colour palette in the borders would be from soft peach to dazzling coral and any shade in between, incorporating flowers such as crocosmia, roses, poppies, irises and lilies.

There must also be water: she remembered seeing basin-shaped containers for dwarf water lilies at a London flower show a few years ago. Once she was back online again, she tracked the company down and one was duly ordered.

By mid-July, the transformation was complete, ready for relaxing days in her oasis of contemplation.

It took a while for Maria to realise that she hadn't seen a single bird in the garden. There were butterflies, bees and other busy insects but no birds. She could hear they were close by and saw plenty in the trees and hedgerows on her walk to the village shop. Providing them with a tempting feast, in strategic places round the garden she hung containers with peanuts, seeds and dried mealworms – yuk!

Day one, two, three… nothing had been touched, but then, stepping out early morning with her cup of tea, she saw that all the mealworms had been eaten. That must be one hungry robin.

Topping the dish up again, she hoped he would have room for more and maybe pass the word round.

Sadly, later that morning she saw a heavy mob of at least a dozen starlings swoop in and demolished the whole lot in less than a minute. Although she felt that she shouldn't discriminate against the humble starling, it would prove far too costly to keep them supplied in mealworms so her bird banquet just had to be seeds, nuts and suet balls from now on.

Starlings should be respected however, for they do have an exceptional quality of putting on the most mesmerising aerial displays in vast numbers. Every evening at dusk, the skies over the Brighton piers turn dark with the bodies of hundreds of them: an amorphous shape-shifting mass, dipping and rising, up and down, round and round. Maria thought it was amazing that there were never any mid-air collisions sending stunned starlings into the sea: how embarrassing would that be.

This summer was proving to be one of the warmest for many years, and all who came to visit Maria in Colthurst Green loved the new home she had created and especially her beautiful garden. The three roses she had planted for Francesca, Thomas and Daniel were gorgeous: big, blowsy old-fashioned tea roses with wonderful fragrances that perfumed the breeze. Many lazy days were spent with dear friends and family, relaxing with a glass of something chilled. She thought the invention of screwtop wine bottles was a marvel, giving rapid access to the contents within. The downside was that, unlike a cork, the top could – and maybe should – be easily replaced, but there wasn't much chance of that happening on a summer's evening with her friends.

The walk up an old Sussex lane into the village always brought the gentle sounds of a slowed down life to Maria's ears. Birdsong creating a pure symphony of sound. She had little hope of identifying which bird produced which song, only blackbirds seem quite happy to sit in a prominent place to put on a show and they really are very tuneful.

The Church of St Nathaniel's dated back to Norman times as part of it had the shape and size of a stone church dating from 1100, or maybe earlier. Large windows indicated the mediaeval builders had learned how to bridge wider openings without weakening walls which have to bear the huge weight of the roof. How clever they were to achieve this without computers and other technological devices to do the calculations for them. Maria was quite sure no modern-day builder could cope with such a challenge with just the aid of a plumb line.

At the west end of the church was a soaring tower arch with walls four foot thick. A stone staircase within the walls leads to a belfry and the roof from which the views of the countryside were stunning.

Maria saw a request for volunteers on the flower rota. Perhaps she should sign up but she wasn't sure of a reconnection with the church yet. Whatever faith she'd had disintegrated and fallen away in the aftermath of Daniel's death when her rage at the world dismissed the possibility of a divine being who loved her. If that were so, how could she have been made to suffer until she shattered into a thousand pieces?

Chapter Three

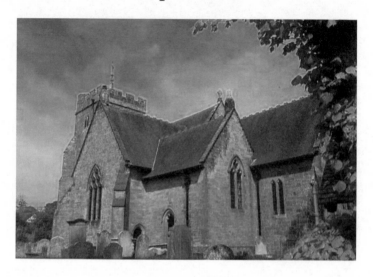

Late August: the time of year when the sun was a little lower in the sky each day and evening shadows lengthened. Maria was now settled in Colthurst Green and she was ready to search out new opportunities to occupy her days. Keeping busy was the best way to distract her thoughts from straying back to a time when a shroud of despair had brought such sadness.

Francesca, Dominic and Thomas had come down for Sunday lunch in her local pub and the topic of how Maria should integrate herself back into gainful employment had come up.

'Well, you've really enjoyed developing your lovely garden Mum,' said Francesca. 'Why don't you check out the local garden centre for part-time work or maybe volunteer at a National Trust garden?'

Maria didn't really want interaction with the public at large and wasn't sure that she needed the commitment of a regular job just yet. Ever the businessman Thomas said that it didn't make great economic sense to do someone else's gardening for free, but he was missing the point that she had to have a focus to every day – something to get up for; occupy her body and mind. She accepted that her days of being a practice manager in a busy doctor's surgery were behind her but maybe her skill set could be used somewhere.

'I was thinking of finding out more about bereavement counselling,' said Maria. 'I'm sure I could help people who are struggling as I did with anxiety and trauma.'

'Oh Mum, don't you think it would open wounds that have hardly healed?' Francesca was worried that her mother was underestimating the time needed to think objectively about grief.

'It's really not a great idea Mum,' Thomas enforced his sister's view. 'Why involve yourself in other people's misery? You need to be uplifted not dragged down.'

Maybe they were right, Maria thought but she did feel a bit deflated.

'Well let's put that on hold while we check out the dessert menu.' Dominic intuitively saw the subject needed to be changed and she quietly thanked her son-in-law for deflecting the conversation.

After they'd gone and Maria was sitting in the garden, watching a couple of bats flitting above her as dusk fell, her thoughts turned back to what new activities best give purpose to her day. She had enjoyed being part of the flower team in St Nathaniel's and their harvest display had been greatly complimented. Kate had taken her under her wing and Maria had been made to feel very welcome. In fact, all the villagers she had met had been friendly and no-one probed into her background more than what she considered polite. Understanding how hard for some people to know what to say when, asked about her family, she said she had three children but one had died and quickly moved the conversation on.

Keeping her religious doubts to herself, she found the Sunday services comforting and calming and the fellowship warming. It was a young congregation and many of the services that summer had included a baptism. There had even been an adult baptism in an enormous paddling pool set up next to the pulpit but unfortunately, it had sprung a leak during the first hymn so a surreptitious mopping up operation had to done while the rector gave his sermon.

Maria had always loved to sing and it was with sadness she realised that hymns were the first time she'd sung since Daniel had died. Grief had brought a silent stillness and discovering the joy of singing was just lovely.

*

'Dad looks a bit pale,' Maria said to her mother at their pre-Christmas family party in early December. 'And he's very quiet.'

'Well, he left his hearing aids in his trouser pocket and they went through the wash so he can't hear much.' Her mother was obviously a bit aggrieved by this.

Eighty-seven, what a great age to live to thought Maria. The changes her dad must have seen in his long life; things her children just took for granted – television and DVDs; microwave ovens; space travel; CDs; mobile phones; the internet and so many more technological inventions that Maria herself hadn't got to grips with yet. Her parents had lead such full lives, even more so in their retirement years that seeing her father slowing down was sad: she thought they would always be there, rock solid in her childhood home.

'Dad really loved Christmas,' said Maria's sister, Amanda. 'Do you remember the time when he festooned the living room with streamers and one by one they all came adrift like a collapsed maypole!'

'And the balloons deflated,' said Maria. 'But that's because he didn't knot them and the string came loose.'

'He was being thrifty and economical, hoping he could use them again the next year. That's what living through a war teaches you.'

She had a point. They lived in such a disposable world now, she wouldn't dream of darning socks, saving gift wrapping paper to re-use or keeping a button box. Her mother had always been pleased to follow the postman up the road, coming home with several discarded elastic bands round her wrist. She would be thrilled to find a coin on the pavement, even just a penny. Maria seriously doubted if she herself would bother expending the energy to bend down to pick up 1p.

The adorning of the Christmas tree was a well-established family ritual and started with their father getting the fairy lights to work. This involved much twiddling of tiny filament bulbs until eventually they all lit up while Maria and Amanda danced round the living room swathed with multi-coloured tinsel garlands.

On Christmas Eve, their dad took them to collect their grandmother from the station where she'd be waiting clutching her little black suitcase with the hinged clasps in one hand and a large bunch of parsley for the stuffing in the other. Maria wondered what the other travellers on the train must have thought of this unusual bouquet, but at the time it seemed quite normal.

At some point in the afternoon, their father would go upstairs to wrap the couple of presents he'd bought for their mother. This always proved to be an incredibly time-consuming exercise, taking far longer than it did her mum and granny to make mince pies; sausage rolls; bread and cranberry sauces; wrap streaky bacon round chipolatas and prunes; peel and chop carrots, potatoes, parsnips, sprouts etc. and stuff the turkey! All the while, trying to keep two excitable little girls under control.

Thomas and Daniel adored their grandfather and, with limitless patience, he kept them amused for hours when they visited. He rigged up a football net for them and made a miniature putting green. He would push them round the garden in a wheelbarrow, and let them help him water the vegetable plot. Maria always made sure she took a spare set of clothes for the boys for not only were they likely to get very muddy but after the much anticipated bonfire they smelled like a couple of smoked kippers.

Francesca was more than happy having granny all to herself. She loved looking at the old photos of Maria and Amanda as children; being taught to knit and 'helping' in the kitchen. They still recall the trifle that had added crunch after she tipped half a tub of hundreds and thousands on it instead of a light sprinkling.

*

Each December released again the overwhelmingly sad memories of Daniel's death.

Would time ever heal her pain?

Probably not; Maria just had to let the anniversary pass, focusing on Francesca and Thomas for it was their tragedy too. Christmas Day itself was particularly tough: it seemed as if she was looking for her lost child. Where was he?

Francesca and Dominic were hosting this year and Maria would drive up from Sussex on Christmas Eve to stay for a few days. A request to bring some parsley for the stuffing wasn't forthcoming; it's too convenient to buy readymade now.

Thomas collected the grandparents on his way down from London and Maria thought how frail her father looked as he was helped out of the car. With great reluctance, he was using a walking stick now and made slow progress up the drive.

After a magnificent festive feast, they all settled in the cosy living room to open presents. When the last ones had been opened, Dominic tapped his port glass and asked for everyone's attention.

'Oh no, he's not going to make a speech,' groaned Thomas.

'Well, yes I am as it happens so listen up. Frannie and I have another present for you all, but you're not getting it until early July.'

'We're having a baby!' squealed Francesca, at which point, both Maria and her mother burst into tears.

Chapter Four

Incessant rain for days and days made for a dismal start to the New Year but Maria's joy at the prospect of becoming a grandmother couldn't be dampened.

For such a long time, Maria hardly dared think there would ever be good news and sense of foreboding darkened parts of every day.

What other tragedies lay ahead that would again unleash the deluge of fear and complete helplessness? It felt as if she was constantly on high alert; ready to brace herself for disaster.

Now a fresh sense of purpose kept her focused on the future and seeing the absolute delight on her parents' dear faces knowing they would be great-grandparents was wonderful: they were all just so elated. This forthcoming little bundle of joy would be a ray of sunshine for everyone in the family.

Her father had been devastated by Daniel's death.

'How can it be right?' he'd implored, with tears streaming down his face.

'Here am I, a useless old man when Daniel had his whole life ahead of him.'

Utterly heartbroken, he would have done anything to have been taken in Daniel's place, leaving his beloved grandson to the life he should have had the chance to live.

Over the years, Maria had learned there was no point looking for reasons where there were none. Life was not just; desperate sadness touches every family.

After another restless night where crazy dreams had spun her round and round in a haunting maelstrom: blurring the edges of reality, Maria forced herself to get out of bed and face the day.

Preparing her breakfast, which these days was nothing more than a simple bowl of cereal, she thought back to when Amanda and she had squabbled over a yellow plastic hippo or some such object of desire. When was it that manufacturers had stopped putting toys in cereal boxes?

No doubt this 'nanny state' of ours, with its excessive health and safety concerns, had banned these delights with the makers terrified of creating choking hazards that would lead to litigation. Good job a well-known burger outlet had continued with their enticements for a Kidz Meal + toy had kept her three occupied on many an afternoon in the long summer holidays. Well, surely she deserved a break from being Head of Children's Entertainment for an hour or so every now and then.

Colthurst Green had been exactly the right place for her to settle down in and begin again. Although she had heard of the village, she'd never visited before. Fate had drawn her there and some things were meant to be. Maria was really very content.

Much to her delight, she had acquired three surrogate nieces in Kate's daughters who were frequent visitors. Annie was seven, Rosie, ten, and Lizzie a very grownup fifteen. They were all so sweet-natured but with very different personalities, reminding Maria of Francesca at various stages of her childhood. She was glad to have the excuse to once again buy craft kits for making cards, bead bracelets, sticker mosaics etc., just as she did when Francesca was a little girl. Gentle afternoons were spent with her 'nieces' busy creating at her kitchen table while Kate and Maria chatted about this and that.

Another good friend she had made was Tracey Bovey. How funny, Maria had thought at their first introduction and with commendable restraint, had resisted asking if she'd been conceived in the Devon town of her name reversed. A question Tracey had no doubt been asked a thousand times and it really can't have been funny the first time.

UK place names could be a bit random. Maria had often thought how great it would be to live in Westward Ho! simply to put an exclamation mark in your address. There was a village called Ripe, fairly near to Colthurst Green and she could well have imagined what Thomas would have said if she had moved there – none of it complimentary or repeatable.

Then there were the Slaughters in the Cotswold: beautiful villages with such gruesome names. There was a Pratt's Bottom near her childhood home town; now, you would really need a sense of humour to live there.

Travellers from abroad must really struggle with the pronunciation of some of our weird place names:

Keighley, where the 'gh' is sounded 'th'

Keswick, where the 'w' is silent (why bother putting it in?)

Marylebone, where even the station announcers aren't sure how to pronounce it.

'Mum, how would you say g-h-o-t-i?' Daniel had once asked her.

'Goatee,' she had said.

'No, it's fish,' he had said triumphantly.

'How did you come up with that?'

Puffed up with self-importance he had said:

'gh' as in cough, 'o' as in women, 'ti' as in station. Fish.'

She had to admit he was right; therein lay the mysteries of the English language.

Deciding to cook herself a proper lunch, Maria fancied a nice spicy chilli and rooted through her cupboard for the necessary condiments. Not for the first time, she wondered why it was that whenever you bought spices they have a sell by date years into the future, but when you come to use them, they're at least three years out of date? The conspiracy of spices was a force to be reckoned with.

True enough, when she found the chilli powder behind the cayenne pepper and the cumin seeds, it was four years past its Best Before Date. Oh well, she'd take a risk.

Another thing that frustrated her was the way food manufacturers send you on some sort of treasure hunt to find this elusive BBD…

See on base

See on lid

See on side of packet

Why didn't they just repeat the date all over the jars and packets?

As her thoughts took her this way and that on spices and BBDs, the phone rang.

'Maria, it's Amanda. Dad's collapsed and been taken to hospital.'

A cold rush of fear fizzed like sherbet in her head.

'Oh no. What happened?'

'Mum found him lying in the hall when she got back from her book club. He must have hit his head on the hall table, there was blood everywhere. I'm just leaving for the hospital now. Mum's worried about you driving up from Sussex, so please don't rush to get here – we'll see you later this afternoon.'

'Tell Mum I'll stay over with her tonight, she must be very badly shaken.'

'Yes, of course.'

'And tell Dad I'm coming and I love him.'

Dear Dad, please hold on till I get there.

In haste, Maria packed an overnight bag and left messages asking Francesca and Thomas to call her on her mobile. The drive up to Kent was frustratingly slow but at last she was pulling up in the hospital car park. She found her mother and Amanda waiting in the corridor outside the ward.

'Oh Maria.' Her mother fell into her arms. 'I should never have gone out. He didn't look right this morning at breakfast. How could I have left him?'

'Mum, you weren't to know. The doctors know their stuff and he's in the best place.'

Maria found herself saying the usual platitudes when you really don't know what else you can say.

'I found out that the paramedics were wonderful,' Amanda said. 'His blood pressure was critically low but they stabilised him and got him on a drip – he was very confused and dehydrated; doesn't seem to know how long he was lying there.'

'What's happening now?' asked Maria.

'They're running some tests on his heart. The doctor we saw said something about breathing difficulties as well.'

After what seemed such a long wait, Maria heard the doctor speaking words that she struggled to process…

…ECG was inconclusive… being treated for pneumonia… course of strong antibiotics… must remember he's a very frail old man…

Seeing she had missed calls from both Francesca and Thomas, Maria went outside to phone them to break the news.

They and Dominic were at the hospital by early evening, by which time their grandfather was sitting up in bed, his head impressively bandaged, eating a chocolate mousse.

'Grandpa, you gave us such a scare,' said Francesca.

'Yeah, talk about attention seeking,' joked Thomas.

'Sorry for all the fuss,' and playing down his own predicament, her father asked Francesca about the baby and whether Dominic had seen the rugby.

'When are you off to Seattle Tom?'

'Not sure Grandpa. The date's been put back a few weeks.'

After an hour of animated family chat at his bedside, Maria said 'Right, come on everyone, let's leave Grandpa to get some rest.'

'We'll come again at the weekend,' said Francesca.

'Oh, I'll be home by then but I won't be pushing any of you round the garden in the wheelbarrow for a while!'

'Gramps, you haven't done that since we were six.'

In the dark stillness just before night gives way to the next day, her father quietly slipped away from this world. The nurse who had been with him assured them it had been quick and peaceful: a dignified ending for one of life's true gentlemen. He had touched lives; how he would be missed.

Grandpa's on his way Daniel. Watch out for him.

Chapter Five

Maria was watching from the upstairs window as the hearse slowly turned into the road. One of the undertakers got out and, with cane in hand, he walked solemnly in front, bringing her father back to the home where he'd lived for nearly fifty years. She wouldn't be saying goodbye to him today for, like Daniel, he would always be all around her, comforting and reassuring.

The family all wanted the service to be uplifting and joyous: a long life celebrated. Francesca and Thomas read loving tributes to their grandfather, as did Amanda's daughter, Abigail. Their mother chose the hymns and Dominic asked for a song to be played that would always remind him of his father-in-law. As Louis Armstrong's gravelly voice filled the crematorium with 'What a Wonderful World', Maria smiled – this was exactly the send-off her dear dad would have wanted. Family had been everything to him and how poignant that as one of its members died, so another was soon to be born into it. This time, it was done in the right order.

Both Maria and Amanda watched over their mother for weeks after the funeral and were on hand if she faltered. They could not begin to imagine how much she missed their father: life must be so different without her partner of many years shaping her day. Being active with many interests, she had good friends who rallied round, but there were still huge chunks of time when she was alone.

Maria knew the daily phone calls she made to her mother were much anticipated; Francesca, Thomas and Abigail were also good about keeping in touch. Although she put on a good show of coping well, Maria knew her mother struggled to find a purpose to her day and, not surprisingly, at times sounded very low.

It had, therefore, come as a surprise that Maria answered the phone one morning and heard her mother's voice upbeat and excited.

'I have such thrilling news for you Maria!'

What could it be?

'Dad's solicitor has come across a trust fund I knew nothing about. It was set up for you and Amanda years ago to be paid out on his death. It really is a huge sum of money and will be released quite soon.'

'Oh wow!' said Maria. 'Dear old Dad, he's still holding us close to him – all he ever did was think of us.'

This really was an unexpected and wonderful last gift from her father and she was determined to use it in significant ways rather than let it be absorbed in household necessities. He would have wanted her to have adventures, create memories, explore new horizons and embrace different experiences. She'd always fancied one of those cooking holidays in Italy or Spain. It was certainly something she would contemplate doing solo as there would probably be other like-minded singletons in the group not looking for anything more than good company and similar interests.

May would be a good month to go; any later and Mediterranean countries would be far too hot for her. Sweltering in searing heat on long ago summer holidays, Maria was resolute in not venturing abroad in June, July or August: May and September suited her much better.

Into the search engine went 'cooking holidays in Italy' and loads of options pinged up on the computer screen. Sifting through them could take a while but one in Sicily immediately caught her eye. Having visited mainland Italy many times with various lovers and husbands, Maria thought somewhere slightly different would be a good choice.

Of course, the sales pitch didn't stint on the superlative, but Sicily really did sound lovely. The pace of life slow and friendly; historical riches were there to be discovered – temples, churches and medieval mosaics. Cuisine was familiar Italian with hints of Arabic spices (she hoped the BBDs were checked regularly). Miles of vineyards; endless olive groves and forests of shiny citrus fruits. With average May temperature of 24° it all sounded perfect – Maria was sold!

Narrowing her search, she found Hotel Cammarata near Cefalu on the northern coast, about an hour's drive east of the capital Palermo. It was a working olive farm about a five minutes' drive from the town centre, which offered cooking holidays very much as guests of the owners Paolo and Sophia.

'It sounds just great Francesca! It's something I've thought about doing and wouldn't dear grandpa approve of me having a little adventure in his memory.'

'Wonderful Mum, book it up now!' Francesca was so glad at how spirited her mother sounded. She had been worried that, having retreated into village life, her mother had lost some confidence and was relieved to think her sparkle was coming back.

Later that afternoon, Maria called Francesca again. 'All booked! I fly out on the 6th May for seven days of Sicilian gastronomic teaching from Sophia. I'll be back well before Bump makes an appearance.'

'You're going to have a fab time Mum. It's such a good idea to have a real break and you may meet someone *special* on the course.' Francesca teased.

'Now stop that! After Matthew, love is not on my radar whatsoever. I'm not going to jeopardise my calm, settled life to accommodate a male of the species and their various demands.'

'OK Mum, I hear you loud and clear! Dom will be so pleased to hear about your holiday. We'll take you to the airport – no arguments. Call you later in the week. Love you lots.'

Had Matthew been a mistake? Maria's second short-lived marriage hadn't been a complete disaster for he had made her feel alive and desirable. After so long on the shelf, it was nice to be taken down and dusted, so to speak. In the beginning, they'd had great fun together; exciting days out and loving nights in. She remembered the comfort of being held in his arms and gentle gestures of loving kindness.

Daniel's death had completely devastated her; she knew she had become unloving and withdrawn: damaged, and it was permanent. Perhaps Matthew's infidelity wasn't wholly unexpected, but she couldn't forgive him. From time to time, she wondered whether she had thrown the proverbial baby out with the bath-water, but without trust or respect, there was no going back.

*

With quiet subtlety, the mild winter blended into spring. It seemed as if they hadn't really had a proper winter this year, with the absence of a single snowflake in Sussex and only a few frosty nights. So different from the past two years which had brought the heaviest snowfalls that Maria could ever remember. With drifts of over two foot deep, she remembered trudges to the local pub with Matthew; games of darts and a bottle of a mellow Shiraz.

The local kids' attempts at building snowmen were really quite pathetic as they rushed their constructions in order to retreat to the warmth of their bedrooms and their comfortable electronic make-believe lives.

There was what Maria imagined to be a 'war-time spirit' as, dressed as snow walkers, neighbours she hardly knew knocked on her door asking if she needed milk, bread, butter, sugar. (Perhaps they thought she had a sudden urge to make bread and butter pudding?)

No cars could venture out of their cul-de-sac as surrounding roads were impassable and without any traffic noise, there was absolute quiet. This gave Maria and Matthew permission to batten down the hatches and watch back-to-back recordings of *Midsomer Murders, Morse and Poirot.*

Of course, the novelty of immense snowfall had worn off after a few days as commuters struggled in to work and schools insisted they were open.

Maria's garden budded with the snowdrops and daffodils she had planted in the autumn; later followed by hyacinths and tulips. Most exciting was that the little birds were slowly coming back, tempted by the food she had lovingly set out for them. A pair of coal tits were regular early morning visitors and a wren had put in a brief appearance. One morning, Maria opened the blind to see a greater spotted woodpecker sampling all the delights on offer before flying up to drill into the pergola. As it was made of super dense heat-treated wood, he soon gave up on that idea.

Pottering round the local town, Maria had seen in the window of a charity shop, a plea for volunteers at the Hospice where her dear friend, Lorna, had died. The memories of six years ago flooded back of how she had watched the cancer overwhelm Lorna's fragile body; her dear friend fighting until the last, until she had no strength left; such a dreadfully painful ending for a beautiful, vibrant lady. She was devoted to her four children, who were of similar ages to Francesca, Thomas and Daniel, as families, they had spent many days out in the school holidays with all the children playing happily together, leaving the mums to catch up on their news.

For a long time after her death, Maria was distressed to find herself thinking that she hadn't heard from Lorna for a while she must give her a call...

Maria had assumed her contemporaries would always be around, as her children would be.

Was there a reason why the advert caught her eye? Maybe this would a good opportunity to step into the world again or at least dip her toe in the water. She scribbled the details down on a scrap of paper and later that day, she called the volunteer coordinator and arranged a meeting.

Driving down the narrow lane towards the Hospice, Maria thought how tranquil and serene the setting for end-of-life care. On visiting Lorna, she had seen doctors and nurses being so tender and attentive in their professional care. Wonderful support and comfort which had extended to the families and friends of their patients.

Parking up, Maria stopped for a moment to take in the amazing view that stretched over fields and woods to the South Downs. She felt that Lorna was around her and hoped she was taking care of Daniel. Maria knew that she had become far more spiritual in recent years, having lost three people who were so very dear to her. It was reassuring to hope that death wasn't the end and those who have loved you will watch over you and love you still.

Chapter Six

Francesca's words about meeting a 'special someone' kept creeping into Maria's thoughts. It would be nice to have a 'gentleman caller', someone to take her out for dinner or for a day by the sea. Would there be anyone to enhance her life, not drain her; drag her down again? She found she was beginning to look at men when she was out and about, wondering if she had it in her to sustain another relationship again. Acting totally out of character, she had actually found herself flirting with the attendant at the petrol station who was very good-looking – and very young.

Previously, having tried and failed to remove the dust caps on the car tyres in order to check the pressure, she thought she would ask for help the next time she filled up. While waiting to pay, she glanced over at the rows of chocolate bars and sweets that could be found in every petrol station across the land. Who buys those packets of sticky sesame snacks? There was also the customary rock hard peanut brittle (otherwise known as 'Dentist's Delight'), and bars of garish pink and white striped nougat which tasted nothing like the real stuff from Montelimar, so beloved of her late Uncle Ray.

Max, as his name badge announced, gave her a dazzling smile as she stepped forward to the till, his perfect teeth showing that he hadn't indulged in much peanut brittle as a youngster. He really was handsome in an old-fashioned, matinee idol sort of way. Maria had always found the dark hair/blue eyes combo very appealing and he was tall with the slimness of youth before beer and too many takeaways take hold.

'Is there someone who could take the dust caps off my car tyres? They've been put back so tightly after the last service, I just can't manage it.' Maria slipped into the 'helpless little woman' role with ease – well, Max was extremely attractive.

'Yes of course. There's no-one waiting after you, so I'll pop out. Move your car over to the air machine.'

'Oh, thank you. That's so kind of you.' Was she simpering?

Max made quick work of twisting off the dust caps. 'I can see why you had trouble, they were on very tight.' His blue uniform shirt stretched over his muscular back as he hunched down (rugby player?) and she noticed an unusual double crown on the top of his head.

'I haven't seen you here before.'

Good grief – did she really just say that??

'I'm back from uni for the Easter hols.'
'That's nice, where are you studying?'

Oh for goodness sake, get a grip Maria, he's not interested in making small talk.

'I'm at Edinburgh in my third year of dentistry.'

Hence the lovely teeth, thought Maria. Who would trust a dentist with bad teeth?

'I hear it's a beautiful city and...'

'So sorry. Another customer; got to go.'

'Thank you, again.'

Maria watched him run back inside. Some girl was going to be very lucky to end up with the gorgeous Max.

*

The clocks going forward made a real difference to the evening light at this time of year, Maria thought as she sat in the garden until gone seven.

Was she missing a male companion?

She had so many lovely social occasions with girlfriends these days, did she really want the complications and chaos a man would surely bring to her ordered life? But the lovely Max had provoked quite a reaction in her; dormant desires were stirring up. OK he was far too young – and, no doubt, thought she was positively antediluvian – but if there was someone special out there, how would she go about finding him? She felt too young for the bowls club or the U3A and the usual forums of university or the work place were no longer options.

None of her friends had tried matchmaking lately, which was probably a relief as there had been a disastrous attempt many years ago before she met Matthew when a friend set Maria up with her husband's cousin. He was a nice enough man but so dull: conversation had stuttered to a halt after half a cider when she just couldn't pretend to be interested in his mountaineering exploits a minute longer. You would have thought he'd scaled the north face of the Eiger instead of Snowdon the way he went on and on. It could have been nerves, but he was the most awful bore and, glad to not have committed to dinner, Maria scooted home as soon as she could.

So; it has to be internet dating, Maria thought as she came indoors and shut the blinds. She knew it no longer carried the stigma of years ago when a brave friend had tried it and concluded it was either for oddballs or for married men who wanted a bit on the side. Maybe she had just been unlucky.

Pouring herself a glass of wine for Dutch courage, she logged on to a well-known site and was off on a virtual adventure.

Daniel, if you're close by, look away now!

Firstly, she had to create a profile, so she used her middle name and took five years off her age (doesn't everyone?). Some of the questions made her smile as she ticked 'a few extra pounds' – a few extra stones, more like. It still remains a mystery how she ever managed to upload a photo of herself for being a total computer Luddite, this was something she'd never done before!

Thanks for that, Daniel.

It took ages to complete her profile (hesitating over including the words 'mountaineers not considered'), and finally pressing 'submit' she wondered if there would be any interest next time she logged on – all this effort better be worth it.

*

'You were so sensible to have done away with a lawn,' Dominic said to Maria as they were having a family farewell lunch for Thomas before he headed off to the States for eight weeks' work in his company's New York office. He was doing so much traveling abroad these days and seemed to thrive on it.

'I'm fed up mowing the grass already and it's only April,' Dominic bemoaned. 'I've got at least another six months of it in front of me.'

'But we must have a lawn for Bump to play on,' said Francesca.

Maria loved to see how her darling daughter was glowing in her sixth month of pregnancy. It was such a special time for a first-time mother – and first-time grandmother: Maria couldn't wait to hold her little grandchild in her arms.

She was quite surprised that Francesca and Dominic had decided not to know the baby's sex.

It didn't matter for not being much of a knitter, Maria wouldn't be making colour coordinated cardigans or bootees anyway.

'Are you going to be there mopping Fran's brow when Bump makes its appearance?' Thomas teased his brother-in-law.

'Well, it's preferable to being down the business end,' laughed Dominic.

'Don't you think it was better in the olden days when fathers-to-be paced the corridor outside the labour ward, then went and got drunk with their mates after the sprog arrived?' said Thomas.

Their conversation carried along in this vein for a few minutes before Francesca exclaimed loudly:

'I am sitting here and pregnancy hasn't made me deaf as well as fat! It may be a huge joke to both of you but I'll be working bloody hard – it's not called labour for nothing. It's more work than you two will ever have done in your lives!'

Oh dear, Maria realised that they'd gone a bit too far.

'That's enough boys! Francesca is bringing the most wonderful gift to all of us – the first member of the next generation. You should put her on a pedestal and worship her.'

'Thanks Mum,' said Francesca, at once enveloped in a bear hug by Dominic who smothered her face in kisses saying, 'We do, we do, oh precious one,' and Thomas made as if to kiss her feet.

*

Putting out the washing the next day, Maria thought how much more optimistic she felt – with real hope for what lay ahead instead of absolute dread of what fate had in store. Maybe she should check the dating website and see if there had been any interest. Bending down to pick up a peg she thought did anyone else find it impossible to hang out the washing without dropping at least half a dozen pegs. Then, instead of just taking another one from the bag, she was obliged to retrieve the fallen peg rather than waiting for it to be joined by others and then picking them all up together. Was there some hierarchy of pegs that couldn't be breached?

Logging on to her laptop, Maria was genuinely surprised to see that she had seven 'smiles' and two emails from prospective dates. However, she soon became somewhat disillusioned as the first 'smile' she checked out had uploaded a photo of himself, which was undisputedly a selfie taken in a gent's toilet judging from the urinal in the background.

The next one loved himself so much he had uploaded no fewer than nine photos in various poses! (Glasses on, glasses off – that sort of thing.)

After rejecting three more 'smiles' the remaining two looked promising so Maria 'smiled' back.

Opening the emails, there was one from Edward, who wanted to take things slowly by swapping emails and photos. She wasn't so naïve as to not guess what sort of photos he wanted, besides, she didn't want a virtual relationship – a computer can't hold hands.

The second email was from Michael who gave his mobile phone number asking her to call him *ASAP* as he was free all weekend and couldn't wait to meet her as they had so much in common.

How desperate was he?

Thinking that perhaps this internet dating lark wasn't for her, Maria logged off and set about planting the rhododendron she'd bought in memory of her father. That was much more satisfying.

Chapter Seven

Money, tickets, passport: Maria did the essential inventory waiting for Francesca and Dominic to arrive to take her to Gatwick for her midday flight to Palermo. Flights times were so sensible, both out and return. Gone were the days when foreign holidays on a budget began at 5am and involved having to watch the Great British public drinking pints of beer and wolfing down a full English breakfast at some ungodly hour, just because they could.

Before going to bed, she had read through the details of her week's stay at Hotel Cammarata. Each course had a maximum of eight guests and the holiday included five days of cooking tuition, both morning and afternoon, and two optional day trips to Palermo and Agrigento. Sophia and Paolo's son, Rafael, as well as doing the airport runs, would act as their guide on these excursions. Maria had already decided she would definitely go on both the trips, soaking up more of the Sicilian culture and cuisine while she was there.

Seeing Francesca and Dominic pull up on the drive, she did a final quick check round the house then opened the front door.

'All set Mum?' said Francesca.

'Absolutely! I'm so looking forward to my holiday. Thanks for taking me to the airport.'

'Is this it?' said Dominic, eyeing Maria's modest-sized suitcase in the hall.

'Yes, I decided to travel light with what I understand to be a holiday 'capsule' wardrobe.'

'You're going to have to tell Frannie how it's done. Every time we've been abroad there's been a real possibility of paying for excess baggage – and then she doesn't even wear half the stuff she's packed!'

'Well, you have to prepare for all eventualities,' said Francesca, piqued.

The trip to Gatwick was swift and soon they were arriving in the short stay car park.

With a moment's nostalgia, Maria remembered that the last time she had been at Gatwick was with Matthew as they flew out to Majorca. It had been a happy holiday but now that seemed like a lifetime ago.

Francesca and Dominic saw her safely through to departures.

'Have a wonderful holiday Mum. Send me a text to let us know you've arrived safely.'

'Enjoy yourself Maria,' said Dominic 'We'll be here to meet you in a week's time.'

After hugs and kisses, Maria went through passport control, towards her much anticipated adventure.

Buying a coffee and pastry after a cursory look round duty-free (it wasn't what it used to be), Maria kept an eye on the monitors, watching for her gate number to come up. Boarding was efficient and only five minutes after the scheduled departure time, Maria's plane soared up into the skies over Sussex.

*

As the plane began its descent into Palermo airport, Maria saw vast fields of yellow flowers and rolling green hills, with a rugged coastline surrounded by the deep blue Mediterranean Sea. It looked just beautiful.

Without any delays at baggage reclaim – unlike with other holidays that had involved tedious waits for their assorted family suitcases to come through – Maria walked through customs (which, for some reason, she always found really hard to do with anything that resembled nonchalance) and immediately saw a stocky young man holding a board which said Hotel Cammarata.

'Buon giorno. I'm Maria Drake. Are you Rafael?'

'Good afternoon Maria. Yes, I'm Rafael. I hope your flight was comfortable. You are the first guest through, so please to take a seat here while we wait for the others to join us.'

What a relief, thought Maria, his English was almost perfect for she'd read that most Sicilians spoke only their own language.

With all eight guests accounted for and introductions made, Rafael led them out to the minibus and they set off for Cefalu.

Maria thought they must look like a motley bunch of travelers as the minibus bowled along fairly empty roads. She was sitting next to Harvey, an elegant older man (sixties?) and judging from his attire – beige, light-weight suit, white cotton shirt with contrasting cravat and tan loafers with no socks – was very much used to being in sunny climes. Maria wondered what had enticed him to come on the cooking course.

Behind them were Agnes and her daughter, Jennifer, who was getting married in the summer. This was probably their last 'mum and daughter' holiday which had evidently been a fixture in their calendar for many years.

Then there were two sisters (Maria didn't catch their names) who looked in their mid-thirties. They were on a culinary mission for dishes to include on the menu of their Bistro in Fulham.

Finally, there was a couple whose four children had bought the holiday for them as a fortieth wedding anniversary present.

During the days that followed, Maria would no doubt find out more about her fellow 'cookees' and hoped that Francesca wouldn't be too disappointed that there didn't appear to be a special someone in the group.

Harvey was charming company on the journey to Cefalu; Maria summised he was gay for he had said a cooking holiday was something he and his partner, Lionel, had talked about taking together before Lionel had died two years ago. Maria didn't want to ask more just yet, but felt she had met a kindred spirit who would understand something of what life had thrown her way.

Through the minibus window Maria saw the endless neat rows of grapevines and the vast groves of knarled olive trees that she'd read of in her guide book.

En route, Rafael pointed out places of interest and gave sound-bites of Sicilian history. As it was in a strategic location in the Mediterranean, it became a battleground for warring civilisations with the Greeks, Romans and Normans all leaving their mark on the island. There were also impressive art collections ranging from Byzantine and Baroque to Arab and Spanish. Medieval streets had been laid out like mazes in old towns like Siracusa and Ragusa where winding alleys were lined with outdoor markets. Sicily's oldest tourist site was the Valle di Templi, where you could wander freely among the monumental ruins.

With all this going on in one small island, Maria thought that a week wasn't going to be long enough.

Sophia and Paolo were waiting to welcome them to Hotel Cammarata, leading them off the minibus to a shady courtyard for refreshments. There were thin shells of crunchy pastry filled with ricottta, almond biscotti and lemon granita, all of which they would learn to make during their stay.

'This really is a perfect setting,' said Harvey as he handed Maria a glass of the granita.

'It all seems so well organised, they've put a lot of thought into the running of things,' said Maria. 'I'm glad that Rafael's wife Gabriella helps with the cooking lessons – her English is as good as Rafael's, unlike Sophia's!'

After refreshments, they collected their luggage from the vestibule and were shown to their rooms which were basic but clean. The good thing about her capsule wardrobe meant that there wasn't a great deal of unpacking to do and soon she was back downstairs, having a look at the beautiful views all around the hotel down to the bay.

Agnes and the girls from Fulham were out on the terrace (perhaps they too had packed capsule wardrobes) and Maria joined them as Gabriella brought out glasses of Sicilian white wine and dishes of plump olives.

After the other guests appeared and had their aperitifs, Paolo led them through to the rustic dining room for a delicious typically Sicilian meal, serving different wines with each course. Talk flowed easily with her fellow guests and Maria found herself feeling very relaxed, knowing that this was just the sort of holiday she needed to give her confidence as she stepped out into the world again.

Chapter Eight

Looking out from her bedroom window the next morning, in the distance amongst the red-roofed buildings Maria could make out the Norman cathedral which dominated the town of Cefalu. The light was so clear and there was the particular Mediterranean island smell of pine and citrus which brought back memories of so many other holidays. If only someone could exactly capture that smell and use it to manufacture the sort of reed diffusers she liked to use around her home. The exotic sounding concoctions she bought never quite lived up to their names; the orchid and mimosa one she bought recently was so nauseating it was relegated to fragrance the outdoor wheelie bin.

After breakfast, Gabriella and Sophia met all the guests in the courtyard to give an overview of the next six days. The excursions with Rafael would be on day three and day five, with the other days devoted to cooking with them in the big kitchen each morning and afternoon, preparing food which they would all eat together for lunch and dinner in the dining room. Part of the old buildings had been knocked through and converted into a cookery classroom with eight work stations, all fully equipped with utensils, cooking pans and an array of oils, condiments, nuts, seeds and jars of candied fruits.

When she booked this trip, Maria knew it wasn't so much a budget holiday as a supreme indulgence, but she could see that it must have cost a great deal to set up the kitchen here and all food and drink were included.

'Andiamo! Off we go to the kitchen for your first lesson.' said Gabriella. 'This morning we make calamari fritti, arancinette all'Olmo and torta al pistacchio.'

Crikey, thought Maria, they were going to be kept really busy.

Sophia and Gabriella gave effortless demonstrations of each dish and, starting with the torta, they all got to work. Each of them would make enough for two persons for lunch which would be shared with the olive farm workers as well as their hosts.

As Maria prepped up the calamari rings, she thought of her dear friend Susan who, full of malapropisms, referred to situations as damp 'squids' instead of 'squibs'. Feeling it would be rude to correct her, Maria never had so damp squids it was – as were the ones slipping through her hands now.

There was a lovely atmosphere in the kitchen as she and the others got to grips with the recipes.

'How big should the balls be?' said Jennifer as she made a start on the arancinette.

'You're the one getting married.' said Jo, one of the Fulham girls. 'How big do you like them?!'

Cue much raucous merriment from everyone!

Harvey and Richard (one half of anniversary couple) were quite competitive in their culinary productions, but she, Agnes and Mary (other half of anniversary couple) were relishing the chance to take their time; cooking for pleasure rather than family demands.

The Fulham sisters made copious notes and asked Gabriella for precise measures of the ingredients in each dish, Maria was more cavalier with the addition of herbs, spices and flavourings – and very generous with the addition of any liqueur!

As the first session ended, Maria was quite pleased with her achievements; although she was glad her dishes weren't going to be offered up for appraisal as on *Masterchef,* with the judge's often crushingly acerbic comments.

With pride, they all carried their dishes through to the courtyard table under the trees where they were all joined by the farm workers for a convivial lunch.

After siesta time, Rafael had offered to take those who wanted into Cefalu for a look round before the afternoon class began at 5pm. They drove past the long sandy beach into the old town with its pretty main piazza. Shops and cafes spilled out into the streets and trattoria verandahs overlooked the bay. They had an hour wandering round and a coffee in the piazza before Rafael took them to the other side of the headland to La Rocca where there was a small marina beyond which Maria could see inlets and rocky coves.

It really was a lovely place to have come to and booked completely at random – maybe Daniel and her father had providing a guiding hand. She liked to think so.

Back at Hotel Cammarata, their next lesson began promptly at 5pm and they would be making melanzine imbottite in sugo piccante, pasta con pesce spada and sorbetti di fragole.

As with their communal lunch, dinner was great fun with sixteen of them round the huge dining room table. Unlike at lunch, Paolo had put at least half a dozen bottles of wine on the table and all were 'well refreshed' by bedtime.

*

Day three and it was the day trip to Palermo. Maria and Harvey sat next to each other again and she learned more of his life with Lionel as the minibus followed the rugged coastal road to the capital.

Leaving school after his O Levels, Harvey had started work as a tailor's apprentice in Lionel's shop in Jermyn Street in the late 1960s. The business had been in Lionel's family for several generations and so far they had fought off competition from high street chain stores, providing a bespoke service for longstanding clients.

Harvey said he had been an awkward, introverted teenager but was comfortable with Lionel's kind and patient tutelage, drawn to the calm, reassuring manner he showed to both customers and his staff alike. He knew Lionel was gay and Harvey began to question his own sexuality for although there had been sweet girl called Anne that he'd taken to the cinema a few times, gradually he realised he was falling in love with Lionel.

One Friday evening, the two of them were working late to finish an urgent suit alteration for a wedding the next day. As they left the shop, Lionel had gently laid his hand on his shoulder and Harvey said that it felt like the wind had been knocked out of him, sending shockwaves from his head to his feet. Lionel had said how impressed he was by how quickly he had progressed since joining the business and what an asset he was. As it was late, he asked Harvey if he would like to join him for a light supper in his apartment in Bloomsbury Square.

'Of course, I said I would love to.'

'Good for you Harvey.' said Maria. 'Why play hard to get?!'

'My life began that evening.' said Harvey. 'I know it's a cliché, but it was like the last piece of a jigsaw had slotted into

48

place. I went for supper and never really left. Lionel asked me to move in with him and we were so happy together for over forty years. We had wonderful holidays and weekend city-breaks; Lionel's friends were all great fun and being gay became less and less of a stigma. Although, we had to put on a bit of a charade when Lionel's mother came to visit and one of the bedrooms was referred to as 'Harvey's room'. As I was nearly fourteen years younger than Lionel, she assumed I was the lodger but, being as sharp as a tack, in time she knew how much we meant to each other and worked it out for herself. Nevertheless, the charade was maintained until she died.'

'So you and Lionel both had a love of cooking?' said Maria.

'No, I did all the cooking and it was dear Lionel's idea for us to have a cooking holiday so he could cook for me after he retired and I was still working. He was keen for me to take over the running of the shop when he was ready to step down.' At this point, the grief in Harvey's voice was palpable. 'He made me promise that I would do all the things we'd talked about before he died and not withdraw from the happy world we had created for ourselves. So I'm here – and thanks to lovely people like you, Maria, I'm having a nice time: it's what Lionel would have wanted.'

'Oh Harvey, how difficult it must be for you now.'

'No, not really. I imagine that Lionel is here with me and I can still share my thoughts with him, like you do with Daniel and your father.'

Maria had told Harvey about what turbulence life had thrown her way as they sat on the terrace the previous evening when all the others had retired for the night.

'It really does help doesn't it.' she said to Harvey. 'I guess people process death differently, but you and I seem to think the same way and have found it comforting.'

Chapter Nine

The hour long journey to Palermo went quickly and soon Rafael was parking up near the centre.

He gave everyone a map of the city and helped them mark on it exactly where the minibus was parked and also some nice trattorias for lunch.

'I hope you all have a wonderful day in this magical city and please be back at the minibus by 5pm.'

Jo and Emma were keen to hit the shops and boutiques. Maria, never really having had a love of shopping, couldn't think of anything worse, but Agnes and Jennifer said they would join them.

Anniversary couple having read, learned and inwardly digested their travel guide, had a punishing agenda for their day in Palermo. Maria doubted very much if they would achieve half of it in the six hours, but judging from the looks of determination on their faces as they set off, they were going to have a damn good try.

'Maria my dear,' said Harvey. 'Would you think it very rude of me to say that I'd prefer to go off on my own to quietly explore the city. It's just that...'

'Harvey, you don't need to explain. I too would prefer some time to be own with my thoughts while I take my time to visit the places that have caught my interest in the guide book.'

'How about we meet up around 4m for coffee and a *dolce* at the pasticceria over there to share the experiences of our day?'

'That sounds perfect! We can talk about what we've seen over something very sweet and sticky!'

Palermo was a colourful, pulsating city with noises and smells assaulting the senses at every turn. The varied architectural styles reflected the historical changes of Sicily's past and the street markets were more reminiscent of North African souks with vegetables, fruit and spices spilling out of huge wicker baskets and a vast assortment of woven rugs and kilims hanging up.

Maria made her way to the Palatine Chapel to see the beautiful carvings and paintings. She thought she would then go onto the Monreale Cathedral to see the stunning gold-leaf ceiling mosaics much enthused about in her travel guide.

However, one attraction that held no interest for her whatsoever was the macabre Catacombe dei Cappuccini which was essentially a human library of mummified corpses. That really didn't make for comfortable viewing in her opinion and it was said it wasn't for the faint-hearted – of which Maria was certainly a fully paid up member. How bizarre that, over the centuries, around 8,000 Sicilians chose to have their bodies preserved in this ghoulish way. The catacombs were badly bombed in the 1940s and many corpses were destroyed but there were still enough on public display for those who were strong of stomach.

By 1pm, the temperature was very hot and Maria retreated to a shady piazza, finding one of the trattorias that Rafael had recommended. She ordered the fish couscous and grilled vegetables and, with a large glass of white wine in hand, she did a bit of 'people watching' waiting for her food to arrive.

Thinking about what Harvey had told her about his long, loving relationship with Lionel, once more Maria thought how precious life is and the most should be made of every moment.

'Well, did you see all you hoped to?' asked Harvey after they had ordered coffee and a selection of the most delicious looking pastries.

'Yes I did,' said Maria, 'and now I'm absolutely knackered!'

'I know what you mean.' laughed Harvey. 'I'm not used to being on my feet for so long anymore. I better rest up before our next trip to Agrigento.'

'Not sure that'll be possible, Harvey, we've got six hours of cooking tomorrow!'

They sat companionably sharing the highlights of their time in Palermo until they saw the others arrive back at the minibus and it was time to set off back to Hotel Cammarata.

Sending a text to Francesca that evening, Maria was thrilled to be able to tell her what a wonderful time she was having and – making sure she told Francesca he was gay – of the special friend she had found in Harvey. At this time in her life, he was so much better for her than what seemed to be coming her way on the dating site for with him there were no expectations of anything other than good company and intelligent conversation.

*

Day five and it was off across country to Agrigento. In her guide book the night before, Maria had read that it was a major tourist attraction due to its rich archaeological history.

The Valley of the Temples is a huge sacred area where seven Greek temples were constructed in the 6th and 5th centuries BC and are some of the best preserved ancient buildings outside Greece.

Rafael said he was first taking them to the archaeological museum which displayed many artefacts from the ancient city so they would get an idea of its history and, after an hour or so, he would drive them to some of the more popular sites. He told them that Agrigento had been established as long ago as 580BC by Greek colonists, becoming one of the most affluent places in Sicily. It was ransacked by Carthaginians around 400BC before the Romans came to capture it around 200BC. After the fall of the Roman Empire, there was more warring from invading Saracens, and then it was fought for by the Normans.

'Good grief!' said Maria to Harvey. 'Haven't the people of Agrigento had to cope with mighty conflicts over the ages!'

'Sounds as stressful as trying to walk down Oxford Street on a Saturday afternoon!' replied Harvey.

After leaving the museum, Rafael took them to see Valle dei Templi which Maria thought was incredibly impressive. Harvey seemed most knowledgeable about the Doric style of building but maybe he had just genned up on it in the guide book.

The temple attributed to the goddess Concordia was in remarkable condition for such an ancient building and the whole atmosphere gave Maria a real sense of days gone by.

Seeing the ruins at Agrigento reminded her of a trip to Pompeii with her first husband in the early 1980s, before children had come along. It had been good to be allowed to wander freely amongst the ruins without being hurried along by officious guides. The Cambridge Latin course she had studied for O Level at school was vividly brought to life for the first part was based in Pompeii around the time of the eruption of Vesuvius in 79AD. The main character was a banker called Caecilius and his ruined house can still be seen. She still remembered phrases like Caecilius est in horto.

Metella est in atrium. Meanwhile, who knows what their teenage son Quintus was getting up to with the handmaidens while his parents spent so much time in the garden and hall!

Rafael then drove them to a number of medieval and Baroque buildings, where, at each one, Anniversary Couple hopped out of the minibus to take his and her matching photos in front of each monument (Mary by the Santa Maria dei Greci; Richard by the Santa Maria dei Greci etc., etc.)

They ended their trip at a gelataria, where they ate the most delicious Sicilian ice cream served in a sweet brioche-type bun. Not for the first time, Maria thought that it was a good job for her waistline that she was only here for a week considering the vast amounts of delicious food she was putting away.

*

All too quickly the last evening came and she was packing her case ready for departure to the airport the following morning. Email addresses had been enthusiastically exchanged after dinner but she knew that the only person she would keep in touch with was Harvey.

Thank you Daniel and Dad for guiding me through this wonderful holiday in Sicily.

Francesca and Dominic were waiting by arrivals to meet her and exclaimed how well she looked – and so brown! Maria was sure that the Bump had grown bigger in a week; she would soon be a grandmother.

Chapter Ten

The days following her return home were filled with warm thoughts of Sicilian days and happy memories of being in the kitchen at Hotel Cammarata.

The leaden Sussex skies and sudden cloudbursts compared unfavourably to the beautiful weather in Cefalu but at least she didn't have to water her garden, which was lush with all the rain. Her father's rhododendron looked magnificent in full bloom, as did the azaleas. Without the risk of a cold snap, she would have to get on planting up her tubs and hanging baskets ready for a splendid summer show.

Thomas wasn't due back from New York until early June. She had missed him but his sporadic emails had told her all was well. On several occasions, Maria had wondered why there was never the mention of a girlfriend – after all, he was thirty next year. Apart from the kooky girl with the 'alternative' dress sense that he'd taken to Francesca and Dominic's wedding, he hadn't brought anyone along to a family get together since.

From a young age, both her tall, good-looking sons had girls queuing up to find favour. Daniel had loved all the attention but Thomas, with his tremendous work ethic, said he was putting all his efforts into making a million by the time he was thirty-five. Judging from the hours he spent at work, it looked like he might just do it. Maria supposed that there was, therefore, little available time or energy to cultivate relationships.

Or maybe he was gay?

He could be and hadn't found the courage to tell her yet.

Did Francesca and Dominic know?

She would have a chat with Harvey when she met up in London with him in two weeks' time on how she could broach the subject delicately with Thomas. She and Harvey had already swapped several emails and he'd invited her up to London for an exhibition at the Royal Academy, followed by afternoon tea at Fortnum and Masons: what a perfect way to spend an afternoon.

Knowing that she would be with Francesca quite a bit this summer once the baby had arrived, Maria wondered how she could spend some quality time with Thomas. Perhaps they could have a few days away together later in the year?

Ever since watching *The Snowman* over and over again as a little boy, he had been entranced by the aurora borealis, so, if it wasn't deemed 'uncool' to go on holiday with mum, maybe a trip in search of the Northern Lights?

It was most definitely on Maria's wish list and it would another adventure that her father would have been thrilled to have funded.

Making herself a salad before she headed off to the Hospice for her afternoon doing the flowers, Maria was most surprised that the 'peel here' instruction on the packet of ham actually cooperated – a rare thing indeed. As she chopped up some beetroot, it amused her that todays' chefs seemed to think they'd discovered this item of food judging from its recent prominence on fine dining menus.

Not so: she remembered long ago Boxing Day cold turkey lunches where sliced beetroot always took its place alongside the other salad ingredients. It even had its own special fork with splayed silver tines and an ivory handle. Now you see it chopped into mini-cubes and arranged artfully on oblong plates, along with a *reduction* or *jus* – listen up chefs, we all know they're just sauces with fancy names.

It amused Maria that when Thomas got back from his various trips abroad, having been wined and dined in exclusive restaurants, the meal he most wanted was Mum's roast dinner!

Maria had been going to the Hospice one afternoon a week since getting back from Sicily – it had taken that long for references and DBS checks to come through. It had surprised her how stringent the process was compared to the part-time jobs she'd had as a student where it seemed if you could spell your name you were in. Perhaps it was a reflection todays' society these where for all sorts of reasons, no-one must be taken at face value.

Rather than discount them for customers, a large national supermarket had taken to leaving out-of-date bunches of flowers by the back entrance and Maria really enjoyed creating small arrangements for the patients' rooms. Unlike in hospitals, flowers were welcome in the Hospice, as were family pets. It was completely understandable that patients needed to see their cats and dogs as much as their relatives and friends – in some cases, perhaps more so.

Combining her love of flower arranging with a sense of purpose was ideal for Maria. Although the Hospice should have been a place of sadness, it didn't seem that way at all. There was a real closeness to Lorna and a feeling of calm control; of having emerged from a vacuum of despair – finally.

Although some of the patients' rooms were overflowing with beautiful flowers, there were always places around the Hospice where Maria could put her arrangements.

'Are you a trained florist?' the visiting sister of one of their younger patients asked, as Maria put an arrangement on the bedside table. It was always hard to see people in the Hospice preparing to be taken before their time – like Lorna.

'No, I just love flowers,' replied Maria.

'My daughter is getting married this September and the quotes we've had for flowers are ridiculous. I don't suppose you do weddings?'

'Well, I haven't done yet,' Maria replied. 'But there's always a first time. It's just me at the kitchen table though; I really couldn't take on too much.'

'It's quite a low-key wedding, just forty guests. The ceremony will take place in the Town Hall and they've hired the function room for the reception. Outside caterers are doing all the food and drink. All we need is someone to do the bride's bouquet and some buttonholes and about six table decorations plus a big one for the top table.'

Was this something she could do? Maria wondered. She was certainly very interested.

'I know, why don't I give you my number and you can ask your daughter to call me for a chat,' said Maria.

Introductions were made and her daughter, Jess, would be in touch.

Driving home, Maria had all sorts of thoughts of bouquets, buttonholes, ribbons and bows running through her mind. Yes, she would do it: what an exciting project for her! Not seeking to make a profit, she would keep the costs really low so that Jess would accept her quote. In fact, whatever she charged would be far, far less than any professional florist and how lovely to be involved in a joyous occasion. Although Maria's two marriages were more than enough for her, she still believed in the institution and it worked for many, as reflected in her parents' long and happy union of nearly sixty years.

Chapter Eleven

Jess phoned the next day, sounding really keen about meeting Maria.

'Mum told me she saw your lovely arrangements when she was visiting Auntie Clare yesterday. Do you think you'll be able to my flowers for the wedding?'

'I'm sure I can. What's the date in September?'

'Saturday 20th. I think Mum told you it's a fairly small 'do' and we'll need my bouquet, about six buttonholes and the table decorations.'

'Yes she did. What are your colours?

'Cadbury's purple and ivory.'

Oh my, thought Maria, there weren't many flowers she knew that came in the deep rich purple wrapper of what had been Daniel's favourite chocolate. Possibly lisianthus?

'Let's meet for a coffee in town and you can tell me the sort of bouquet you'd like and I'll bring an example of the sort table decorations I make.'

A date was set to meet up with Jess, and Maria once again thought how frequently life sends you off at tangents; you're doing one thing which then leads you off into another.

In her more reflective moments, she had likened life to a lily pond with herself on one lily pad and all her family and friends on other lily pads around her. Sometimes by choice and at others times by force, you moved from one lily pad to another. When Daniel died, her familiar, safe lily pad was rocked so much she fell off into the dark, fearful waters beneath. Her friends had come across the pond and helped her to climb back on, but things did not look the same anymore. An empty lily pad where Daniel should be: it would always be there.

*

Mid-June and a heatwave was baking the south of England as Maria drove up to have Sunday lunch with Francesca and Dominic. Thomas would also be there and it would be the first time Maria had seen him since he got back from New York, but it certainly wasn't the occasion to ask him if he was gay. Harvey had said it was not the sort of thing that should be dropped into a conversation, nor should it turn into a summit meeting. His advice to Maria was to wait until Thomas himself was ready to say something – if indeed there was anything to say.

'Phew, what a scorcher!' said Dominic as he opened the door to Maria. 'Frannie is so uncomfortable in this heat.'

'I can imagine.' replied Maria. 'Still, not long to go now – three weeks?'

Yes, the midwife thought about that judging from how Bump is lying.'

Maria went through to the garden where a hot and bothered Francesca was sitting under a large parasol with her swollen feet in a tub of water.

'Oh, my poor little girl! How are you coping? I hope my lovely son-in-law is keeping you supplied with cold drinks and ice creams.'

'Hi Mum. Yes, Dom's being an absolute treasure – I couldn't get through these days without him.'

Again, Maria thought how lucky there were to have Dominic in their family. His care and concern was so reassuring; he was keeping them all safe.

'Look at me! I didn't think it was possible to get this enormous and my feet are so bloated the only shoes I can wear are Dom's old flip-flops! If this baby doesn't come out soon I think I'll burst.'

'Has the midwife given you an indication of how big the baby is?' asked Maria.

'A *good size* is what she said. What's that supposed to mean??'

'Well, Dominic is over six foot and Grandpa was tall.'

'As long as Bump hasn't got a big head like Thomas you'll be OK.' laughed Dominic.

'I heard that!' said Thomas arriving in the garden by the side gate, clutching flowers, champagne and a gargantuan teddy bear.

'Bump's first present from Uncle Tom.'

'Good grief!' exclaimed Francesca. 'It's five times the size of any baby I'd want to give birth to!'

'How are you Mum?' said Thomas hugging Maria.

She held her son tightly; it was so good to see him.

As with countless times before, they all had a lovely day together catching up on Thomas's work trip (Maria had to hold herself back from asking about the 'nightlife') and news of Dominic's parents who had just holidayed in Cambodia and Vietnam – they were far more intrepid than Maria; Sicily was more than adventurous enough for her.

Maria had bought a very contemporary buggy/carrycot/car seat for the baby – much nicer than anything that was in the shops in the 1980s when she had her little ones. Prams seemed so heavy and cumbersome back then, no wonder her upper arms had been toned. She decided that she would buy several outfits after the birth for, even though the baby already had a fairly extensive wardrobe of non-specific gender clothes, it would be nice to do the traditional blue/pink thing once she knew the sex. She'd also seen some wonderfully inspiring baby toys – although, what babies seem to like best of all are a set of shiny keys and the TV remote.

Back home in Colthurst Green, Maria turned the page in her diary to see what the following week had in store. She was building a new and satisfying life and, now that she had been here over a year, the steadying process was safely underway. All she needed to do was remember that which had helped her through the worst of times and stay focused on the path that lay ahead.

Chapter Twelve

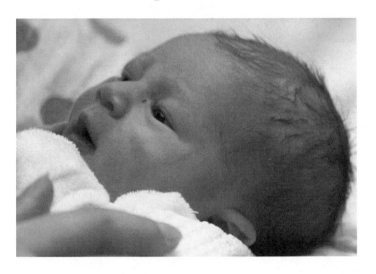

'Hello Granny!'

Maria answered the phone to Dominic early one morning in late June. His voice was choked and he gulped, trying to get the words out.

'What? Has the baby been born?!' Maria crackled with tension and excitement. 'It's early! Is it a boy or girl?'

Tears on the other end of the phone.

'Take a deep breath Dominic and tell me what's happened!'

'We've got a baby girl... and she's perfect!' said Dominic in between sobs. 'Frannie's contractions started yesterday morning and then seemed to stop... But late in the afternoon, things really took off again... so we went to the hospital around eight in the evening… and we're told that she was in the second stage of labour… Frannie was so brave and in control and…'

Apart from hearing that they'd called her Evie Danielle, most of what Dominic said was lost as Maria, beside herself with happiness, wanted to shout out loud 'I'm a grandmother!'

Her little granddaughter had come into the world and it was just the best thing that had happened to Maria in a very, very long time.

*

Almost bursting with joy, Maria rang Thomas, her mother, and her sister in quick succession.

'I'll pick you up around midday Mum, and we'll go straight to the hospital. We won't stay long as Francesca will be exhausted. Thomas says he's going to wait to hear from us as to whether when Francesca and Evie will be allowed home tomorrow.'

'Tomorrow? They don't keep you in for long now. It's not like in my day, when new mums had a long stay in hospital after having a baby. I was in for two weeks after having you!' said her mother.

Dominic met them at the hospital entrance and they went up to the maternity ward. The lift seemed to take forever and Maria's impatience nearly got the better of her. Finally, they got to the ward and there, peacefully sleeping in Francesca's arms, Maria saw her tiny baby granddaughter for the first time.

Overwhelmed with emotion, she couldn't speak. Stroking Evie Danielle's petal-soft cheek, Maria heard her sigh; her eyelids fluttered and her little fingers curled and stretched out.

'Oh, she's just so beautiful Francesca! You clever, clever girl.'

'Would you like to hold her Mum?'

As Maria took the precious bundle, the significance of a new life just beginning was immense.

'We had already decided that Bump's middle name would be Daniel or Danielle,' said Dominic.

'Thank you.' said Maria. 'That means so much to me.'

As her mother took her turn for a cuddle, Maria could sense the bittersweet mixture of feelings as she held her great-granddaughter; the thrill of seeing the next generation but also such sadness that her husband had missed this special moment.

'I'm so glad that your dad knew he was going to be a great-grandfather before he died.'

'I know Mum,' said Maria. 'He and Daniel are watching down on us all and they'll keep Evie Danielle safe.'

I just know you both will.

Seeing that Francesca was tiring, Maria and her mother left the new parents to continue to wonder in amazement at the little girl they had made together.

'This was only ever going to be the briefest of visits my love.' said Maria 'and you must rest as much as possible while Dominic's with you.' His company had been generous with their arrangements for paternity leave and Maria was glad that Francesca would have his support during Evie's first weeks.

Maria spent the night at her mother's before coming back to Colthurst Green where she settled down to phone more of her family and friends with the wonderful news.

'I'm so very happy for you, Maria.' said Harvey. 'Thank you for letting me know so promptly. I can imagine that there's nothing like a new baby in the family to lift one's spirits.'

'I can't begin to tell you how amazing it feels to be a Granny! This baby is going to be so treasured.'

Sparing Harvey the grim details of childbirth, they chatted about Evie's arrival and how gorgeous she was before arranging for him to come down to Sussex for a few days the following week.

'Are you sure that you won't want to be with Francesca?' said Harvey.

'I think it's better that both she and Dominic spend the first week or so quietly with Evie, it's such a special time. They'll have Francesca's father, Dominic's parents plus other visitors coming to see our new addition. My turn will come round again and I'll be of more use when Dominic goes back to work.'

Maria didn't want to crowd Francesca and Dominic as they got to know their baby daughter and the steep learning curve that is parenthood.

Chapter Thirteen

Next morning, Maria answered the phone to Thomas.

'Thomas, hello! Have you seen your little niece yet?'

'Yes, I went to the hospital after work yesterday. Isn't she a cutie-pie! Fran's a natural with her and Dom's absolutely besotted! They were being allowed home today.'

While they were catching up on each other's news, Maria thought it would be the right time to mention her idea of going away for a few days together later in the year. Bracing herself for a none too enthusiastic reply, she was heartened to hear Thomas say:

'I'd really like that Mum. It would be great to spend some time with you. Any idea where you'd like to go?'

'Well, I remember as a little boy you were transfixed by the Northern Lights in your Snowman video so how about we go in search of them?'

'Oh wow, I'd really love to!'

'I've done a bit of research and found a four-night package trip to Iceland mid-November. I'll email the details to you and hope it fits in with your work schedule.'

'I'll make it fit Mum.'

That went better than expected, thought Maria as she forwarded the itinerary to Thomas. She wasn't sure why she had been anxious that he might not have welcomed the suggestion of spending time with her. Recognising that for a very long time after Daniel's death, she was so utterly lost in her own desolation that it had been impossible to acknowledge how badly her other children were suffering.

Back then, in order to re-orientate and rise to the surface, she had to concentrate on herself and in so doing, had neglected both Francesca and Thomas. But what else could she have done?

Thomas had said once that he felt so guilty for not looking after his little brother and wished it was him who had died. Horrified that he felt that way, Maria hoped that her words, although in no way adequate, had consoled him a little. Everyone who knew Daniel would have wanted to have done something – anything – to have stopped his life ending so agonisingly and abruptly. She realised that Thomas's way of coping had been to bury himself in his work. Although he had always been driven, he was now bordering on the manic in the hours he gave to the company.

*

Maria scanned the passengers alighting from the London evening train for Harvey's tall, upright frame.

'Harvey!' He was easy to spot, handsome in his linen suit.

Kissing Maria on both cheeks, he said, 'You look absolutely radiant! Becoming a grandmother has done you the power of good.'

'It's so good to see you Harvey. You're certainly dressed for the hot weather we've been having! We've got so much to talk about and lots of photos of Evie Danielle to show you.'

They drove to Colthurst Green with Harvey admiring the Sussex countryside in the warm evening light.

'You've found a delightful part of England to settle in Maria. We went through some beautiful scenery once the train had left suburbia.'

While Harvey unpacked his gentleman's valise (the word 'suitcase' wouldn't have done it justice), Maria looked for a vase big enough for the stunning summer bouquet Harvey had given her. Checking it first for the solitary dead, curled up spider, which seemed to use her vases as their final resting place, she arranged the flowers then, with the Prosecco cork satisfyingly popped, they sat in Maria's garden looking at the photos of her adorable granddaughter.

'Right, time to eat. In honour of our Sicilian sojourn, I've made *carne alla pizzaiola* followed by *crostata di ricotta al forno*! In fact, all the meals I'm cooking while you're here are based on Sophia and Gabriella's recipes.'

'Wonderful Maria! I'm afraid I haven't recreated any of the culinary delights we were taught. Lionel would be so disappointed at my apathy but it's easier for me to stop by at one of the local bistros on my way home from work each evening and I tend to dine out with friends most weekends. I promise I'll make an effort when you come and stay with me.'

Over dinner, Maria outlined the places she would be taking Harvey during his stay, chatting long into the night over the exquisite handmade chocolates and bottle of Muscat de Beaumes de Venise he'd also brought.

What a generous houseguest, thought Maria; he'll be invited again.

Chapter Fourteen

'Today, I'm taking you to Sheffield Park,' Maria told Harvey at breakfast. 'The water lilies should be flowering in abundance right now – I must remember to take my camera – then we'll have lunch in a centuries-old pub in a pretty nearby village. We must go into the churchyard for there are stunning views over the fields and woods of Sussex all the way to the South Downs.'

The water lilies were indeed spectacular, stretching in vast carpets across the lakes with their goblet-shaped flowers in white, yellow and pink standing proud of the lily pads. Ducks and moorhens swam amongst them and a regal pair of swans glided across the lake to where she and Harvey stood.

'I sometimes see myself as a swan.' she said to Harvey. 'Seemingly calm and in control on the surface, but underneath, I've got huge, ugly feet paddling like fury!'

Harvey laughed, 'Life is smoke and mirrors. You never know what people around you have to cope with, doing all that they can just to tread water.'

'There were many, many days when I thought I'd never recover from Daniel's death; each day a Sisyphean nightmare, repeated over and over again.'

'I can only imagine the pain of losing a child.' said Harvey. 'The abject sense of despair and rage you must have had at the injustice of it. The courage it took to keep going for the sake of Francesca and Thomas and the new life you have made for yourself. You are amazing.'

'I won't pretend it was easy.' replied Maria. 'I hit rock bottom and had no idea what I could do to regain stability. Even now, I know I'm fragile and close to the edge at times but I have strategies in place to help me cope.'

'When Lionel died, I couldn't see how I could go on without him. With no joy or reason to anything, I wanted to die too, but that would have been giving up and Lionel wouldn't have wanted that. The melting pot of emotions I was in overwhelmed me: at one point I was incredibly angry with him for leaving me to cope alone, then I'd be so guilty for feeling that way.'

'I know what you mean Harvey. No amount of counselling or medication can stop these thoughts.'

Walking round the park, they continued to chat about the past and present.

'Are you busy in the shop?'

'No, things quieten down as summer approaches then picks up again in the autumn as our regulars update their winter wardrobes. Lionel gave such impeccable service, offering tea, coffee or a generous measure of fine single malt while cloth was selected and styles of tailoring discussed. We have a loyal client base.'

'I'm sure you're keeping the flag flying Harvey.'

'I have excellent staff to support me and I intend to stay in the business as long as I can. It's essential to keep busy and hold close the connection with Lionel. I'd only get maudlin with too much time on my hands.'

Over supper, Harvey said he'd recently rediscovered his love of sketching and painting.

'I always enjoyed art at school, in fact I was rather good. About the only thing I showed any aptitude for, as my teachers were at pains to tell me!'

'Well, that's marvellous Harvey. You must let me see the sort of thing you do and I may commission you to paint a watercolour for me.'

'You're going to think me quite presumptuous, but I've actually brought my sketchbook with me. I've been out and about in the London Squares which Lionel and I loved to visit: such surprisingly green oases nestling in the bustle of the city.'

Maria thought his artwork was really very good showing Harvey had an excellent eye for composition and perspective.

'I know, why don't we go down to the seaside tomorrow and you can sketch a beach scene for me. Also, the chalk cliffs around Birling Gap are quite dramatic. As they're rapidly crumbling into the sea, you'll be capturing a snapshot of time. The coastline will look completely in a few years – that will surely add value to the painting!'

The drive to the sea took just over half an hour from Colthurst Green and soon they were walking down the recently erected wooden staircase onto the pebbles at Birling Gap.

'This is where we scattered Dad's ashes in April. My parents loved this stretch of coast and came here many, many times over the years. They spent their honeymoon in Eastbourne in the early 1950s when it was an elegant and sedate resort. I guess it still is, compared to Brighton!

It seemed such an appropriate place to finally put Dad to rest. What did you do with Lionel's ashes?'

'They're still in the plastic urn provided by the undertaker at the back of a wardrobe I'm afraid. I just can't bring myself to do anything with them.'

'What about taking them to your favourite London Square? I'll come with you if you like.' said Maria.

'Yes, I'll give that some thought, although we had many favourites but I must come up with just one. I've never liked the idea of putting an egg-cupful here and an egg-cupful there. I'd want to keep him as one.'

'When we collected Dad's ashes, there seemed to be some creative alternatives to just scattering like putting some in a glass paper-weight or having them heat-treated and processed into gemstones for jewellery!' laughed Maria.

'A friend of ours wanted his partner's ashes made into a firework and launched skywards, but they were always far more flamboyant and melodramatic than Lionel and me.'

Maria thought that even with such a sad event, a kind of humour would emerge for driving down to Birling Gap with the family in the spring, her mother in a bit of a panic suddenly said, 'Have we got Dad??'

Deciding to place the ashes into the sea, as she and Amanda paddled up to their knees with the urn, Maria nearly lost her footing causing Thomas to shout 'Don't shake him up too much, Mum.'

'Where did you scatter Daniel's ashes?' Harvey gently enquired.

'It was Francesca and Thomas's idea to take them to his beloved cricket ground, the site where in his four years of playing for the 1st team he'd taken numerous wickets and made hundreds of runs. They also asked if they could place a small commemorative plaque in the clubhouse. I go there on my own sometimes and feel incredibly close to my precious boy.' Maria sighed, feeling the familiar sting of sadness from deep within.

After choosing a good view to sketch, Harvey sat down with his drawing book while Maria pottered up the beach looking for shells now the tide was going out.

'Let's see what you've done,' said Maria, returning to Harvey an hour later.

'Oh no, it's going to be a surprise! I've made several preliminary pencil sketches of the cliffs and shoreline then I'll work on the watercolour back home.

They spent two more happy days together before Maria took Harvey back to the station.

'Next time we meet in London you must stay with me in Bloomsbury. I have to warn you that the apartment is nothing like as modern and uncluttered as your lovely home. In fact, my niece and nephew say it's a cross between an old Gentleman's Club and *Britain's Greatest Hoarder*!'

Chapter Fifteen

With Dominic back at work and all associated family members and friends having been to see Evie Danielle, Maria's turn had come round again and this time, she would be spending five whole days with her. Fortunately, the weather had cooled down from the excessive heat of the past weeks to the more comfortable warmth of an English summer. Accompanied by a suitcase full of gorgeous pink and white outfits for Evie and a collection of the latest baby toys, the drive up to Francesca and Dominic's couldn't go quickly enough.

It was only a couple of weeks since Maria had seen her granddaughter, but already she had changed. Evie had lost the crumpled, bewildered look of the newborn and had nicely filled out into her peachy skin. She had a mop of dark hair and her alert eyes were taking everything in.

'Look at her expressive hands and long fingers.' said Maria. 'Maybe she'll be a pianist like Grandpa.'

'She's been so good, Mum; really placid and content. I'm only getting up once in the night to feed her and she settles down again straightaway.'

'Just like you did. My advice is to stop at one and quit while you're ahead.' laughed Maria. 'Numbers two and three are seldom as easy!'

Insisting that Francesca put her feet up, Maria rolled up her metaphorical sleeves and set about familiarising herself with the kitchen and preparing lunch.

'I've offered to run a stall at the village fete on August Bank Holiday Monday.' Maria told Francesca in the garden after lunch.

'Are you sure about that Mum? Our delightful English weather can never be relied upon to do the right thing. I remember that painting you had up in the old house of two deckchairs on the Brighton seafront being lashed with rain. It was called *Bank Holiday Monday* for a reason!'

'Well, I'll give it a go. Granny's coming to stay – she loves a village fete – and Kate and her lovely daughters are helping me. I'm doing it to raise funds for the Hospice where I volunteer. We're making up small floral table decorations, giving demonstrations as we go.'

Maria thought back to all the fetes she'd been to as a child in long ago summer holidays. Her father always had great success on the coconut shy, which was a bit awkward as Maria and Amanda really didn't like coconuts back then. She herself liked the Wheel of Fortune and Hook a Duck best. Also Splat the Rat, which was strange as she wasn't an aggressive child until that paddle was put in her hand.

She remembered her mother winning a five pound note by spearing it with a dart (which was a lot of money back in the early 1970s). The stallholder didn't look too pleased handing it over; probably wondered how his specially blunted dart pierced the top prize.

In Throw a Hoop, Amanda maintained that the wooden rings were always too small to go over the square blocks, although it never stopped her trying her luck. In those days, before the Animal Protection League weighed in, you could still win live goldfish which were hanging up in plastic bags around some stalls. Some of them must have been quite healthy specimens for a goldfish Maria won at Blackheath Fair when she was about ten lived for over thirteen years in a small bowl on top of the fridge.

'I'm so glad you had a lovely time with Harvey.' said Francesca

'He's wonderful company: so kind and thoughtful. I can't believe we only met in May, it seems as if we've been friends forever.'

'It's a bit of a shame he's gay Mum.'

'On the contrary, I'm glad he is. We can enjoy stimulating conversations and spend time together without sex getting in the way.'

'Mother!!'

It made Maria smile that each generation thought they were the first to discover sex – if they only knew!

Maria and Francesca had lots of fun trying all the outfits on Evie. Some, sensibly, had been bought for her to grow into as Maria knew she wouldn't be wearing newborn clothes for very long.

'She's just gorgeous.' Maria said hugging her granddaughter close and smelling the unique fragrance of vanilla and rose petals that babies have around their little necks. 'It's been so wonderful to have spent this time with her – and you, of course, my own little baby girl!'

Before Maria went home, a date was fixed for them to come down for Sunday lunch in a few weeks.

'I hope Thomas can come as well – he was really smitten by his little niece.' said Maria.

'He sounded very excited about your trip to Iceland, Mum.'

'I thought it would be nice for me and him to spend time together before he finds himself a girl and settles down.'

'Not much chance of that happening anytime soon. He's enjoying the single life too much!'

Hmm, did Francesca know something she didn't?

Chapter Sixteen

August Bank Holiday weekend and, as Francesca had predicted, the weather forecast was dire. Maria had driven up to Kent and collected her mother on the Sunday and they drove back to Colthurst Green through several heavy cloudbursts.

'These squalls are supposed to carry on into tomorrow,' said her mother, 'What a shame after all the effort people have gone to for the fete, including yourself Maria.'

'We're British Mum! The show will go on whatever the weather throws at us.'

Over to you Daniel and Dad. Bring out the sunshine for us!

The next day, under a grey sky and a distinct chill, Maria and her mother met Kate to set up the stall. They had got together to make twenty or so mini-flower arrangements the evening before and had a couple of buckets with fresh flowers to make up more during the afternoon if the stall proved to be popular. Any leftover flowers, Maria would take to the Hospice where they were sure to be appreciated.

'We could be lucky, those clouds don't look too threatening.' said Kate, as the first raindrops fell.

The light drizzle became a relentless downpour over the next hour and looked set in for the day.

Maria felt so sorry for the girls from a local dance school, one of them being Annie, Kate's youngest daughter. They had obviously practiced so hard for their performance in the arena but with fixed smiles on their faces, slipping and sliding on the wet grass, they went through their routines with grim determination.

She felt just as sorry for the owners of pets in the dog show – even the dogs themselves looked pretty glum as the rain drenched their specially groomed coats.

The jazz band played on regardless under their sturdy marquee (no doubt having played at many a village fete, they knew the marquee would be a sound investment).

The beer tent was doing well, Maria noticed: no surprise there.

'The Punch and Judy man was supposed to be here.' said Rosie, Kate's middle daughter.

'He probably saw the weather forecast and wimped out.' Kate replied.

Maria was pleased that her table arrangements had sold well but with the awful weather keeping spur-of-the-moment visitors away, after an hour and a half of getting soaked – in spite of huddling under Kate's garden parasol – they decided to call it a day.

'Next year, I think I'll just give the Hospice a donation.' an exhausted Maria said to her mother after a hot shower and a large gin and tonic. 'It will cause much less angst.'

*

As if to rub salt into the wound, the first days of September were glorious – sunny and warm with clear blue skies. The blackberries looked ripe and juicy as she walked down the lane. Was it really too much to ask for just one fine day for the village fete?

Oh well, Maria was pleased to have raised over £100 for the Hospice and, as they were self-funding, every pound made a difference.

Jess phoned to say that all her preparations were going smoothly as the big day approached and Maria confirmed she'd ordered purple lisianthus, ivory roses and mixed foliage. She had contacted a local wholesaler, knowing that the supermarket where she generally bought her flowers wouldn't have sufficient quantities for large scale production.

Two days before the wedding, the kitchen resembled a florist's back room as she began sorting out the flowers and cleaning the stems before giving them a conditioning drink overnight.

Next day, she started by making the table arrangements, followed by the buttonholes. Then, with great trepidation, she began the bride's bouquet. The special florist-foam holder she'd bought with the handle for the bride to grip was a first for Maria and it took a while before she felt as if she knew what she was doing. After a good two hours' work, with all the flowers and foliage securely placed and the tiny crystal butterflies added she stepped back and thought it really did look quite professional.

'Oh wow, the flowers look fabulous!' exclaimed Jess's mother when she came to collect the bouquet and buttonholes the following morning. 'You really are very talented. Jess is going to be thrilled with her bouquet – it's absolutely exquisite!'

She introduced the best man and a friend who were going to take the table arrangements straight to the reception room.

'How's Jess feeling?' Maria asked.

'She's fine but she was furious with her husband-to-be yesterday. Daniel hadn't ...'

Daniel?? Her Daniel??

For a moment, Maria felt as if she had been punched in the solar plexus; completely winded, her head emptied of rational thought as the sound of her son's name stopped her in her tracks.

'Are you all right?'

Caught in a moment of lost time, Maria had to force herself back to the present.

'Yes. Um, fine thanks.'

'Anyway, Daniel hadn't tried his suit on again after it had come back from having the trousers shortened and when he got round to it yesterday, they'd been taken up too much and were flapping round his ankles and then...'

Maria hoped it looked as if she was listening to what was being said, but her mind was spinning with the stark realisation that her Daniel would never have *his* wedding suit altered.

The feeling of being cheated out of *his* wedding day and being a grandmother to *his* children.

It was impossible to steel herself for moments like this – they came unannounced; out of nowhere. The anxiety that had suffused her for so long after Daniel's death could tighten its grip at any time leaving her struggling to breathe normally; trapped in a panic attack that would not release.

It wasn't just her son she had lost, but part of her future and she would always rail against the crippling unfairness of what she was left to deal with for the rest of her life.

Chapter Seventeen

September had tumbled into a mild October and she was looking forward to her weekend in London with Harvey, especially autumnal walks round the lovely parks and seeing *Phantom of the Opera*. Harvey had been astonished she said she hadn't seen the stage production, only the film, that as soon as they'd sorted out Maria's visit, he'd booked tickets for the Saturday matinee.

'I'd like to say I disagree with your niece and nephew, but I really don't think I can.' laughed Maria as Harvey showed her round the apartment, which was cluttered beyond belief.

'Ah, but every object tells a story and every book has been read by Lionel or myself at some stage.'

It really was an Aladdin's cave of treasures with all available cabinets, shelves and tables holding precious memories of a happy life shared.

'This was taken on our last holiday together.' Harvey showed Maria a photo of the two of them in Mexico. 'Lionel always had an interest in the Mayan civilisation and we went to some fascinating temples and museums while we were there. It was about then that I started to notice how quickly he got out of breath and struggled in the heat. We didn't know it at the time, but it was the beginning of the end.'

Harvey showed her to her room and Maria quickly unpacked – she was getting good at this capsule-wardrobe style of travelling. The room reminded her somewhat of her grandmother's bedroom with the dark wood freestanding furniture and paisley printed eiderdown. (She very much doubted if her children knew what an eiderdown was, having slept under duvets all their lives.) As with all the other rooms in the apartment, it was crammed full of pictures, books and photographs.

She could see why Harvey couldn't face moving, it would take weeks – months – to pack everything up. There was sure to be hardly anything that he could bear to get rid of.

So different from when she moved to Colthurst Green; clearing out the old house had been quite liberating in some sense. Keeping only what she used or needed had helped her to accept her new life, without being weighed down by unnecessary baggage from the past.

'I'm taking you to a local bistro for dinner tonight. As I said, my culinary skills are woeful now I live alone.'

'That will be lovely Harvey. I'm looking forward to getting to know your London.'

The bistro was almost full as they arrived but they were shown to Harvey's 'usual' table in the window.

'Welcome, welcome my friend, and your beautiful companion.'

'Good evening Roberto. This is my friend Maria from Sussex who's spending the weekend with me.'

'Bella, Bella!' said Roberto, theatrically kissing Maria on both hands.

With their food chosen and the wine poured, they caught up on each other's news and the evening flew by.

Saturday, after breakfast, they went out for a stroll to the local squares: Russell, Woburn, Gordon and Tavistock.

'I didn't know there was a statue of Gandhi here.' said Maria as they sat on a bench in Tavistock Square.

'Yes; Lionel remembered it being unveiled by Harold Wilson in the late 1960s. People of all religions and races frequently meet here to light candles and pray for world peace. Maybe they'll make a difference, but from what I read in the newspaper each day, it's a long time coming. It's ironic that the tragic London bombing July 2005 took place here.'

'What's that big rock over there?'

'It's the Conscientious Objectors Stone, placed there in 1994.'

'How strange. Recently, my mother was talking about a family friend who was a conscientious objector in the war. He was brave in another way though for, although he wouldn't fight, he volunteered for the bomb disposal unit. He diffused hundreds of unexploded bombs by the end of the war, saving so many lives.'

'That was brave.' said Harvey. 'This is probably my favourite square; it has quite a range of historical tributes. Dickens lived here while he was writing *Bleak House* and Virginia Woolf wrote *Mrs Dalloway* – her house was bombed in the blitz.'

They walked over to a bronze bust of Louisa Aldrich-Blake, one of the first British women to become a surgeon; responsible for significant advances in medicine in the early 1900s.

'Would you be allowed to put Lionel's ashes here?' Maria asked.

'Do you know, I've been thinking of that; Lionel was such a gentle pacifist, so against any form of aggression. The Peace Square seems appropriate doesn't it; I'll give it some thought.'

They went back to the apartment for a light lunch before getting the tube to Piccadilly Circus and the short walk to the theatre for *Phantom of the Opera.*

Maria was really looking forward to seeing the musical and there was something about these faded old London theatres that reminded her of a bygone age; although people must have been so much smaller back then, she thought as she squeezed into her seat. Surely theatre architects wouldn't have deliberately set out to make you feel as uncomfortable as possible for three hours or more. Harvey said he always books an aisle seat for himself so he can stretch out his long legs: sensible.

'Thank you so, so much, Harvey.' gushed Maria as they left the theatre. 'That was absolutely amazing! Isn't the music incredible – how many times did you say you'd seen it?'

'About seven or eight – over the space of twenty or so years I hasten to add.' laughed Harvey. 'It was Lionel's all-time favourite; that and *The Lion King* which we took all our nieces, nephews and godchildren to in rotation!'

'We'll have to bring little Evie Danielle to see it when she's old enough.' The thought of taking her granddaughter to a London show was just lovely.

Chapter Eighteen

Sunday, and they took the tube to Green Park. It brought back the memories of the time Maria had been trying to salvage what was left of her marriage to Matthew for they had met up by the statue of the girl and greyhound on a bright, cold December day some years before. Maria told Harvey the story of the disintegration of her second marriage as they walked through the park towards Buckingham Palace.

'Perhaps it was an inevitable casualty of the fall-out of my grief at losing Daniel.' she said to Harvey, 'but I was running on empty for so long – with no end in sight at that time. I gave what little I had to Francesca and Thomas; there wasn't much left over for Matthew.'

'Oh my dear, I hope I haven't upset you by suggesting we start our day in Green Park.' Harvey was worried at the thought of reminding Maria of such sadness.'

'Not at all. I now feel that, since Matthew and I broke up, the way life has taken me is better. I very much doubt if I have it in me to sustain a relationship again; I genuinely don't feel sorry for myself. It's a relief to know that I can cope with everything in my life and enjoy all I have – which is a lot.'

'You've come a long way Maria, and you should be incredibly proud of that.'

Arm in arm, they walked into St James's Park. There was no sign of the pelicans; maybe they had been moved somewhere warmer for the approaching winter. Plenty of other water birds were enjoying the late autumn sun on the lake. No herons though. Those birds had always entranced

Maria, possibly because they looked so prehistoric in flight: you could see that pterodactyls were their ancestors.

They stopped for a coffee in the café before continuing their walk into the Mall and up the steps towards Trafalgar Square. One of her first dates with Matthew was a bitterly cold, early January day in London. It had seemed unnaturally quiet as they walked towards Nelson's Column and they couldn't believe that the fountains had actually frozen over!

She and Harvey made their way into Covent Garden for lunch with Harvey pointing out things of interest at every turn. Living in London for so long, there wasn't much he didn't know. Sitting outdoors under patio heaters, Maria thought that there was always something going on here with street entertainers providing a free spectacle for visitors. Over the years coming here with her young family, they'd seen jugglers, fire-eaters, even tightrope walkers. The human statues had fascinated Daniel and after staring at a silver-painted Roman centurion for several minutes, he'd jumped out of his skin when it moved and tocked him on the head with its spear. Thinking it might give her a moment's peace, she suggested that he and Thomas practice being human statues when they got home: it hadn't worked.

'My dear friends Edward and Charlie have invited us for dinner this evening. They know I don't really cook anymore and wanted to make sure my houseguest wasn't starving!'

'It will be lovely to meet some of your friends Harvey, although you know I would have been happy with a cheese sandwich.'

'They're very special people and were so kind to me after Lionel died. I've told them about how we met and the courage you've shown in getting back on your feet again since Daniel's death.'

Edward and Charlie lived in an elegant townhouse in Bedford Square.

'As you can see, our tastes in décor are a bit more 'minimal' than Harvey and Lionel's.' joked Edward as he showed Maria round.

Charlie was a photographer and framed examples of his work were hung throughout the house.

'These are truly stunning: are they taken in China?' asked Maria.

'Japan.' said Edward. 'We went there on holiday in 2010.'

'And these?'

'The Maldives. Absolute heaven on earth!'

Edward owned an art gallery in Cork Street and invited Maria to pay a visit next time she was in London. Later on that evening, after a superb meal, he said that one of their friends was an exceptional artist who was looking for, let's say, *mature* models for an exhibition she was working on.

'You'd be perfect Maria.' said Edward.

Her? A painter's model? What would the children say?!

'You have a lovely enigmatic and soulful face that tells a story.' said Charlie.

'My body tells a story, too, but that's definitely not for public viewing!' laughed Maria.

'I think you'd find the experience quite liberating Maria. Like an acknowledgement of survival.' Harvey said.

'I'd have to be fully clothed. Thomas wouldn't speak to me again if he saw a painting of his mother in the buff!'

'Well, why don't I take a couple of photos of you and let Christa see them.' said Charlie.

'What now? I'm a bit squiffed and red-in-the-face from all that wine!'

'The abandoned look is definitely *au courrant,* Maria.' said Edward, mischievously.

Much to her surprise, and encouraged by Harvey, she found herself letting Charlie take some photos (she insisted on only head and shoulders) and wondered if this would lead to another new adventure.

How funny: for so much of her life it had been Maria at the helm, now she was letting the tide make the choices – and it was working out all right.

Chapter Nineteen

Maria found a seat at their agreed meeting point and watched the crowds of travellers milling around the airport concourse as she waited for Thomas. No-one looked particularly happy, in fact, quite the opposite as they tried to fathom out the automatic check-ins and scanned the monitors for their flights.

It really wasn't surprising as some of the most fraught moments of her life had been spent in airport departures, marshalling her overexcited children and keeping them entertained throughout unacceptable delays. Francesca had easily kept herself amused with her colouring and sticker books but Thomas and Daniel had been such hard work. Smiling knowingly at a young father whose hyperactive charges were leading him a merry dance, she thought it seemed like a different lifetime when she herself was a parent to three little children.

Thomas arrived and after hugs and kisses, took over the checking in procedures. How lovely to have a handsome, capable son to take care of her.

'I suppose air travel is second nature to you after all your trips abroad.'

'I guess it is Mum, but you never know what delays you might get. The worst one was in Atlanta when the parking brake got stuck after the plane had taxied to the runway for take-off.'

'Oh yes, I remember,' said Maria

'After the engineers spent over an hour trying to release it with the plane surrounded by about eight fire engines, they finally towed us back to the gate and we all had to get off. It ended up with them having to put us up in a hotel for over twenty-four hours while the problem was sorted out, which was pants.'

Fortunately, there were no such calamities today and soon they were settled in their seats chatting about Iceland. Maria told Thomas she had read astronomers were predicting that the Northern Lights should be the brightest in decades right now due to a peak in the solar cycle – whatever that meant. Their package included a four-hour evening coach trip to the best viewing location near Reykjavik on that night, being picked up at 8.30pm from the hotel. (She better make sure she had a siesta that day, she would need to stay awake much later than she was used to – 10pm was a late night these days.) Maria so hoped they would be lucky enough to see the Lights but as they were a natural phenomenon, there was no guarantee.

'We're booked on the tour of the capital tomorrow afternoon where we'll be shown the historic midtown and harbour, also the Pearl with its mirrored glass dome, and Hallgrimskirkja Church... I don't think I've pronounced that correctly,' said Maria. 'I had a go at learning some key phrases from the guidebook but with all those runs of consonants, it's impossible!'

'I wonder if they have the equivalent of our *Countdown* on TV in Iceland?' Thomas pondered. 'It must get a bit repetitive with the contestants saying "I'll have a consonant, please, and another and another one and another one" – brilliant!'

'We're going on the Golden Circle tour the next day which takes in the Geysir geothermal area which has a dozen or more hot water blowholes – I think that's what you call them – and the Gullfoss waterfall which supposed to be incredible. Then onto Thingvellir National Park where your geology A Level should come in handy as it's on the Great Atlantic Rift which is slowly pulling Iceland apart.' said Maria.

'Bloody hell Mum, have you swallowed the guide book? You're very well informed!'

Maria laughed at her son's gentle teasing; it was going to be a lovely holiday with Thomas creating special lasting memories of the days that the two of them will have shared.

'That leaves a free day if you want to do something really adventurous, such as snowmobiling on a glacier or snorkelling through a fissure between two tectonic plates. You could even try scuba diving or hike up a volcano; I know you like to be active!'

'No, it's our time together Mum, and to be honest, the past few months have been so hectic at work, I'm quite inclined to take it easy for once.'

Looking out of her window as the plane made its mid-afternoon descent into Keflavik airport, Maria thought that the view couldn't look more different than from when she landed in Sicily in May. The overall impression was of a dark grey landscape with few trees and hedges. She could see steep ragged cliffs along a rocky coastline and the sea was much paler than the deep azure blue Mediterranean. There were rivers snaking into huge lakes and vast mountainous areas in the distance. Iceland was going to be so different to any other holiday she'd had before: somehow she knew she was going to enjoy the experience.

*

After checking into their hotel, they made their way to their separate rooms. Maria had thought it would be better if they weren't sharing a room; Thomas might want to sample whatever nightlife there was in downtown Reykjavik (which certainly wasn't on her agenda), and she didn't want to be woken up with him clattering into the room at some late hour.

Her room was modern and comfortable with expansive views towards the city. She had read a hotel review that a guest had actually seen the Northern Lights from their room – would she be as lucky?

Guide book in hand, she went down to meet Thomas in the foyer and, obtaining the free bus pass from the concierge that they were entitled to use during their stay, they stepped out to sample the delights of Reykjavik by night.

Chapter Twenty

Opening her curtains the next morning, Maria was so disappointed to see the capital shrouded in misty drizzle. Still, maybe the skies would clear in time for their trip to see the Northern Lights by the evening. If not, no matter, for the deal was that they would have a second chance tomorrow night.

Both she and Thomas had such a lovely first evening in Reykjavik. They'd found a lively diner near the harbour entrance which served excellent burgers (sometimes a burger really hits the spot and they were delicious). They'd got chatting to a delightful Danish family who'd been to Iceland several years previously and had seen the Aurora Borealis in all its glory. Maria was always impressed by how well the Danes, Swedes and other Scandinavians spoke English, but she remembered hearing someone say, who's going to learn their language? Harsh, but true. Evidently, Icelanders aren't used to foreigners speaking their language and find it most bizarre when they attempt to: they almost always reply in English!

After showering and dressing, she went along to Thomas's room to scoop him up for breakfast.

'Hi Mum.' A sleepy boy opened his door. 'I can't believe how well I slept.'

'That's great my love. I wanted you to recharge on this holiday – you've been working so hard.'

'This holiday has been a great idea of yours. Love you Mum.'

'No rush to get ready Thomas. I'll have a coffee and wait for you downstairs.'

Today, they were booked on the afternoon Reykjavik Grand Excursion, a comprehensive introduction to Reykjavik's past and present which took in the Perlan, the old harbour, and the National Museum. Until she'd read up about it in her travel guide, Maria had no knowledge of Iceland's historic past. The Vikings were thought to have built the first settlement around 900AD and one of their longhouses was still in remarkable condition. As well as medieval manuscripts and carvings, artwork and statues, there were more contemporary art galleries and museums to visit during their short stay.

'I'm not sure about these 'alternative' sculptures Mum.' Thomas said as they walked round an exhibition in the gardens of the first museum on their afternoon trip. 'It's all a bit abstract for me.'

'I'm sure they're more impressive on a sunny day; this grey drizzle isn't doing them any favours.' Maria said from under the hood of her waterproof coat.

They both agreed that the Perlan was very impressive with its mirrored dome: a very imaginative building with cylindrical water tanks converted into a tourist attraction. Just a shame the weather wasn't kind enough to let them appreciate the stunning views from the top.

Arriving back at the hotel, there was a notice on reception saying that, due to adverse weather conditions, the Northern Lights trip was postponed until tomorrow.

'Thought it would be.' Maria sighed. 'I hope the weather improves, it will be very frustrating not to have the chance to see the Lights while we're here.'

'Come on Mum, let's go to the bar for a sharpener.' Thomas knew his mother was disappointed.

'Even if we don't see the Lights, there's so much for us to do here, I didn't realise that Iceland was such an interesting place to visit. We must go to the Blue Lagoon – you love a spa and evidently, this is the spa to end all spas!'

'Too right!' laughed Maria, 'but more importantly, it's so lovely for us to spend time together. We haven't done anything like this before and it's been great to hear about what's going on at work and all that's happening in your life.'

Now was her chance...

'Anyone special I should know about?' Maria asked, casually.

'No Mum.' Thomas smiled, knowing full well what his mother was angling for. 'You'll have to wait a bit longer to buy a hat for the wedding.'

'But you are happy?' she was so anxious that Thomas had recovered from the impact of his brother's death.

'I miss Dan: he was my mate as well as my little brother. I feel my guard is always up in case someone else I love it taken away from me. It's made me very cautious about forming a relationship with someone.'

Maria completely understood what her son was saying for god knows she felt the same.

'It's OK to take chance Thomas my love. You cope with risk at work and most of the time it turns out well. Don't be too hesitant about letting someone into your life.'

Sensing that this was enough on this subject for now, Maria suggested they both go to their room for get ready for another night on the town.

'I'm going to see if I can book a table for dinner at the Perlan.' Thomas announced. 'You never know, if the skies clear we may see the Northern Lights from the revolving restaurant under the dome!'

What a thoughtful son she had.

*

On waking the next day, with trepidation, Maria looked out the window. Although the skies were a bit clearer, with some breaks in the clouds, there wasn't a great deal of improvement. Still, they had their whole day excursion to occupy them and Maria was really looking forward to seeing the hot springs and waterfalls. After breakfast, they gathered what they needed for the day and waited in the foyer for the coach to pick them up.

'The restaurant was superb last night Thomas! Thank you again for a lovely meal.'

'It was a bit special. The food was very good.' Knowing that Thomas had eaten in some pretty fine places, that was quite a compliment.

The coach set off on time and they drove through some spectacular scenery on their way to Geysir.

'Did you know that Geysir gave its name to thermal blowholes in general – geysers?'

'You're full of interesting facts Mum. Dan would have been impressed – he always liked a bit of trivia!' laughed Thomas.

They nudged each other when the guide, in his running commentary, mentioned the 'impressive spouts' they would see and the 'reliable Churn' – the highest gusher in the hot springs area. Joking apart, the area really was quite something with slushy, belching pools of mud and an all-pervading sulphurous whiff. Once again, it would have been better on a sunny day but Maria thought at least her expensive waterproof jacket was getting good use.

Moving on, their next stop was the Gullfoss waterfall. Truly dramatic, this two-tier waterfall made an incredible noise, and as luck would have it, the sun made a brief appearance producing rainbow mists as the waters thundered down into the canyon.

'Are you sure you don't fancy some white water rafting Thomas?' joked Maria as they got soaked by the spray, despite the disposable plastic capes provided by the tour company.

'Only if you come with me!' laughed Thomas.

Hmm, although her mantra was to embrace new experiences, Maria thought that may be a step too far.

Their day trip took them on to Thingvellir Park where the coach drove them through diverse scenery from prominent rocky outcrops and cliff-lined gullies to the largest lake in Iceland. They stopped at a narrow flooded lava fissure. It had become a kind of wishing well as glinting coins could be seen in the clear cobalt blue water. Both she and Thomas chucked some krona in and made a wish. While she kept it to herself, her wish was for her beloved son to find peace of mind and happiness of heart. In time, she dearly hoped he would find a companion to walk his path with him.

The ominous presence of the framed notice on at the hotel reception from the Aurora Borealis excursion guide reported that the weather conditions were not encouraging. However, the minibus would still pick them up at 8.30pm in the hope of clearer skies north of the usual viewing point. It would mean a longer drive inland for a better chance of seeing the Lights.

'Right, well I'm going to have a long soak in the bath and maybe a doze – it's going to be a late night and I don't want to fall asleep on the minibus.'

Thomas, who had always been a night owl, knew it wouldn't be a problem for him.

'OK Mum. See you in the bar for a drink and snack before we set off.'

Although their guide and driver did their very best to search for the Lights, they remained elusive above the overcast night sky.

Come on Daniel and Dad – clear the skies for us!

Reassuring the group that conditions can change quickly, especially if the wind gets up Maria could tell that the guide was desperate that they see something. At one point, the outline of the moon was glimpsed behind the clouds: could she see green lights dancing in the umbra? No, nothing more; just darkness.

They got back to the hotel just after midnight. Maria felt a bit hollow; she so much wanted them to share the wonderful experience of seeing the Northern Lights together.

'Oh well, my love, we'll just have to dig out your *Snowman* video and pretend we saw them.'

'Don't worry Mum.' Thomas hugged Maria tightly. 'We're having a great holiday together and have seen some fantastic sights. Your face when the big Churn blew at Geysir was a picture!'

They spent their last day at the Blue Lagoon, lazing in the warm waters of the huge bathing pool. Even though the air temperature was hardly conducive to being outdoors in just a swimming costume, the hot steam released from the nearby geothermal power station kept the water at comfortable body temperature. It was quite an experience for Maria to bob about in powder-blue waters, bordered by rough masses of black volcanic rock with soft rain falling on her face.

Both she and Thomas had booked massages at the adjoining spa, after which they treated themselves to delicious

Icelandic lobster at the restaurant which overlooked the lagoon.

*

Arriving back at Gatwick, Maria and Thomas made their way to the trains to head off in opposite directions.

'Mum, I can't thank you enough for organising such a fab holiday! I feel so refreshed and it's been really good spending time with you.'

'My darling, you've been a wonderful companion. We'll do something like this next year shall we – maybe a European capital city?'

'Absolutely Mum!'

Safely home in Colthurst Green, Maria felt the usual tug of sadness after spending time with someone she loved. Good job there was her trip to see Evie Danielle the week after next.

That was the key to staying on an even keel – having something ahead to focus on.

Chapter Twenty-one

It was the first week in December and the frosts were hitting hard. Good, thought Maria; hopefully they were going to have a proper winter this year. Blanketed in snow, the country lanes around Colthurst Green would look like perfect Christmas card scenes and she relished the idea of cosy evenings in with her lovely friends, hearty food and copious amounts of red wine.

Looking forward to spending a couple of days with Francesca and Evie, Maria realised that she definitely had withdrawal symptoms from not having seen her gorgeous granddaughter for nearly a month. Oh to hug that soft, wriggling bundle of happiness again: she couldn't wait for all those kisses and cuddles.

Feeling smug as she reversed her frost-free car out of the garage, she none-the-less marvelled at the crystalline fern patterns of hoar frost on the windscreens of outdoor cars as she drove out of the estate. How does nature create such complicated designs of swirling symmetry?

'Francesca, you look wonderful. How have you lost the baby weight so quickly? I'm still carrying mine after twenty-five years!'

'Mum, you're gorgeous just as you are! I wish I had your perfect skin.'

'So do I.' said another voice from the living room.

'Abigail! How lovely to see you. I didn't know you were going to be here, what a wonderful surprise.'

'Hi Auntie M.' Abigail hugged Maria. 'Just look at Evie, hasn't she grown?'

Evie had indeed become a real little person since Maria last saw her, smiling and chuckling; lifting herself up on her chubby little arms and desperately trying to crawl. Just seeing her made Maria's heart soar: this precious baby girl had done so much to help the healing process just by being born.

In the kitchen, Francesca hastily told Maria that Abigail was staying for few days as there were 'difficulties' at home. It seemed that Amanda's marriage was rocky, which really surprised Maria for her sister and Michael always appeared so happy and in tune with each other. Evidently, Abigail had noticed a *froideur* after moving back home after finishing university last year, which in recent months had developed into arctic permafrost.

'Abi says they hardly speak to each other.' Francesca told Maria. 'And when they do it's to snipe and find fault. They constantly avoid each other with Uncle Mike always going off to play golf and Auntie Amanda is either at the gym or her Pilates classes.'

This was so sad, thought Maria. In the past, she understood that her sister's marriage must have been sorely tested by the repeated miscarriages she'd suffered before and after Abigail was born. Amanda had always wanted a houseful of children and Michael adored fatherhood. Knowing you were going to become parents and then having that ripped away from you must have been desperately traumatic. Even after they'd had Abigail, further miscarriages can't have been easy to accept; deep in the womb, they were already little beings, longed for and loved.

For most, the dreams and hopes we have for our children are there the moment we know we've conceived. Just as Daniel had been snatched away from her, Maria knew her sister and Michael had coped with similar anguish… again and again. Little lost souls grieved for.

'Would it help if I talked to Abigail?' Maria said.

'Oh yes Mum. I'm sure you'd know the right things to say.'

After lunch, all wearing hats, scarves and gloves for protection against the cold, bright afternoon, they strolled to the local park with Maria proudly pushing her well-wrapped granddaughter in her deluxe buggy. While Francesca sat with a giggling Evie on a swing, Maria and Abigail walked round the lake.

'Can I help?' Maria gently enquired. 'Francesca says things are somewhat strained at home.'

'Oh Auntie M, Mum and Dad are so cold and unloving with each other these days. While I was away at uni and only home for the holidays I didn't really notice; now I'm living there permanently, the atmosphere is awful. It's obvious they don't want to be together anymore – they never do anything as a couple. I feel caught in the middle and it's horrible.'

'Have you spoken to them about how sad it's making you?'

'Not really. I've asked them to be nicer to each other. I know I'm twenty-three and should be renting my own place. Perhaps I'm in the way.'

'No, that's not true Abigail.' Maria was upset that her niece could think that. 'Just continue to lead your own life; you're doing so well with the investment company. Don't let mum and dad's problems weigh you down; they'll find a solution – even if that means separating, eventually. Take it from me; it's a tall order to be in a happy, fulfilled relationship with the same person for years and years. Things will be resolved somehow.'

'As their only child, I feel that should be the glue holding them together.'

'No sweetheart, that's not your responsibility. It's just not straightforward; otherwise all parents would stay together forever. Both you and I know that doesn't happen.'

'I know.' sighed Abigail. 'I just want them to be happy again.'

'They may well be, but that's something for the two of them to work out.'

They walked and talked some more before joining Francesca and Evie to feed the ducks and geese.

'Abi seems a bit brighter.' Francesca said as they were preparing supper later that evening. 'I've persuaded her to stay another night so we can all eat together.'

'We had a good chat in the park and I hope I've reassured her that she's not the custodian of her parent's marriage. Like so much in life, there's a beginning, middle and an end.'

Francesca knew that her mother was thinking of Daniel when she said this. December was a tough month for all of them – it would be nearly six years since he had died.

The mood was lightened with Dominic coming home from work and aperitifs being poured. Maria was so fond of her son-in-law: his absolute adoration for Francesca and Evie was plain to see.

'Christmas is going to be so different without Grandpa this year,' Francesca said, as they were finishing supper. 'Granny must really be missing him; they always did so much in December.'

'I know.' said Maria. 'One year, I think they ate their way through seven Christmas lunches at various festive occasions with Probus, Guild, the Bowling Club etc!'

'Grandpa would still be wearing his paper hat from his cracker when he went to bed!' laughed Abigail. 'He always loved Christmas day with all the family together.'

'Well, that's what we should have this year,' exclaimed Dominic. 'The whole family together with us here for Evie's first Christmas!'

Chapter Twenty-two

'Harvey! How are you?' Maria was always pleased to hear her dear friend on the phone. He'd gone away with Edward and Charlie to their apartment in Portugal about the same time she was in Iceland with Thomas.

'Did you enjoy the Algarve?'

'We were swimming in the pool and grilling sardines on the barbecue everyday – rather different from your holiday in Iceland I imagine, but did you and Thomas have a lovely time together?'

Maria told Harvey of the special time she'd spent with her son, despite not seeing the Northern Lights. They chatted about their respective holidays for a while before Harvey said, 'Now, Maria, after seeing the photos that Charlie took when we went for dinner, Christa is very interested to meet you.'

'Oh… right.' Maria was hesitant. 'I'm really a very private person, Harvey.'

'I know you are, but why don't you meet Christa and see what she has in mind. I'm not familiar with her work: it could be very abstract and Picasso-like – no-one would recognise you with your mouth, eyes and nose moved round your face a bit!'

'OK. Tell Charlie to give her my email address and I'll take it from there.'

Next, Harvey asked her to accompany him to Edward and Charlie's traditional New Year's Eve party, which always had a 'theme'. Phew, this was turning out to be quite a loaded phone call, Maria thought.

'What's the theme Harvey?'

'Well, I think you'll approve, this year, it's movie stars pre-1960. I've already given it some thought, and how about you and I go as Vivien Leigh and Clark Gable in *Gone with the Wind*?'

Yes, that could work Maria thought, relieved that he hadn't suggested Tarzan and Jane – which wasn't surprising for just as she didn't have the svelte figure for Jane, dear Harvey certainly didn't have the excessively muscular physique for the Lord of the Apes. However, he would look very debonair with a Rhett Butler moustache though.

'Lovely. Now why don't you come up to London on the 30th December and stay with me as long as you like.'

'Thank you Harvey. That sounds wonderful.'

Blimey, wait till Francesca and Thomas hear about this – it would be Maria's most exciting New Year's Eve for many years. In recent times, it had been spent on her own with a bottle of champagne, cuddling her dear little dog and watching a repeat of *You've Got Mail* on TV.

*

'What? Naked??'

'Shhh!' Maria quickly looked round to see who might have heard. She had just told Kate about being persuaded to pose for an artist while the two of them were helping the flower ladies decorate the church ready for the Christmas services.

'You didn't have to say it so loud and, no, definitely not naked!'

'Why not? You could be artfully draped with silk and lace.' laughed Kate.

'It's not going to be erotic, so I'm assured. Christa is working on an exhibition to celebrate the mature woman – every face tells a story and all that.'

'Well, I think you should go for it Maria. It will be quite an experience and a lasting image of who you are now.'

They chatted about their plans for the festive season: Kate seemed to have her vast family descending on her, with eighteen people for Christmas lunch. Maria guessed that Kate would be run off her feet for the next two weeks in preparation for just one day.

When she had been at the wheel of the Christmas 'juggernaut' she had genuinely loved those family-filled, joyous Decembers; watching Francesca, Thomas and Daniel, excitement mounting as they counted down the days to Christmas with the doors on their Advent Calendars.

Knowing that she didn't have the stamina for her traditional Christmas shopping trip to London, she made do with the more-than-adequate nearest high street. Evie was easy to buy for and Maria had to hold back on her purchases of toys and clothes lest Francesca would say she was spoiling her. Wasn't that what grannies did?

Francesca and Dominic had requested a bread maker. Maria hoped it would fare better than other seemingly essential kitchen gadgets like juicers and ice-cream makers which, once the novelty invariably wore off were consigned to the backs of cupboards with vases and dead spiders.

Thomas was always difficult to buy for. With his definitive, expensive tastes, Maria didn't dare chose clothes for him, although she was tempted by an amusingly naff Christmas jumper she saw. It would be worth buying just to see the look on his face when he unwrapped it.

The children's letters to Father Christmas had always amused her: Francesca would always ask for crayons, colouring books, stickers and anything creative. Daniel's list was usually exhaustive and wide ranging. One year when he was seven or eight, amongst other things, he'd asked for an *Alan Shearer Supersoaker, Stretch Armstrong* and some 'cool' boy's earrings. (How he proposed to wear the earring without having had his ears pierced was a mystery.)

Thomas was generally more restrained and his list featured anything with wheels. It wasn't surprising that since starting work, he'd driven a progression of sporty cars, whose desirability had risen in proportion to his increasing salary.

Like most parents, Maria had seen Christmas becoming increasingly materialistic since her childhood. From October – or sooner – TV channels bombarded children with adverts for fantastic toys and games that they lives wouldn't be worth living without.

She remembered a friend getting so fed up with her children's greedy demands for extravagant Christmas gifts that one year, she went on the Oxfam Unwrapped website and bought them all a goat for an overseas family living in poverty. When they opened a solitary envelope on Christmas Day thanking them for the generous gift which would make a tremendous difference to an underprivileged family for many years, they were at once disappointed and contrite. Their mother had made her point.

Chapter Twenty-three

It was the anniversary of Daniel's death and Maria had driven back to the town where they used to live. Sitting outside his old cricket pavilion in the bitter cold of a mid-winter's day, she allowed the emotions to flow over her as thoughts were filled with her lost child.

Some young lads were playing football using their hoodies as make-do goal posts. Maria thought they must be freezing as the light dusting of snow got kicked up. She thought she had seen a few snowflakes as she closed the curtains last night and hoped to see a good covering by the morning, but nothing significant had appeared.

Get that snow machine working up there you two!

Watching the dog walkers exercising their charges in the recreation ground, she wondered if now was the time to think about getting another puppy. Although she was sorely tempted, one of the toughest moments of her life had been holding their dear little Westie as she had been put to sleep by the vet nearly three years ago. At fifteen (over a hundred in human years) she was an old lady and her organs were failing. The vet had assured Maria it would be the kindest thing to do, but holding her adoring and adored companion of so many years as her life ebbed away was utterly agonising.

Pain upon pain: how much more could she take?

The bare, black branches of winter trees scratched the heavy white sky and the sparse hedges were dormant. A bold robin hopped quite near to where Maria was sitting and stayed close by for a long time, seemingly respecting her grief.

There was stillness in the air: a quiet, hopeful expectation of what would happen next?

On the drive home, she knew there would be no need to make the pilgrimage to the cricket pavilion next December for Daniel was wherever she was.

Resolving from now on to look back only to see how far she'd come, Maria reflected on what the past year had brought her: as for everyone, there had been highs and lows, but now so much to look forward to.

Evie Danielle's first Christmas would be magical, although she wouldn't remember much about it, everyone else would – especially Maria.

Edward and Charlie's New Year's Eve party would be great fun. She had hired a dramatic red ball gown with a fitted bodice and huge skirt for her role as Scarlett O'Hara and Harvey said he was busy growing a moustache.

Then there were the sittings for Christa's painting coming up in January.

Maria thought she might just do it naked – she really did...

Not The End.